A EUROPEAN PAST

OTHER BOOKS BY FELIX GILBERT

Johann Gustav Droysen und die preussisch-deutsche Frage, 1931

Johann Gustav Droysen: Politische Schriften (editor), 1933

Hitler Directs His War (editor), 1951

The Diplomats, 1919–1939 (edited with Gordon A. Craig), 1953

To the Farewell Address: Ideas of Early American Foreign Policy, 1961

Niccolò Machiavelli e la vita culturale del suo tempo, 1964

Machiavelli and Guicciardini: Politics and History in Sixteenth-Century Florence, 1965

The End of the European Era: 1890 to the Present, 1970, 1979, 1984

Historical Studies Today (edited with Stephen A. Graubard), 1972

Bankiers, Künstler, und Gelehrte: Unveröffentlichte Briefe der Familie Mendelssohn aus dem 19. Jahrhundert (editor), 1975

History: Choice and Commitment, 1977

The Pope, His Banker, and Venice, 1980

FELIX GILBERT

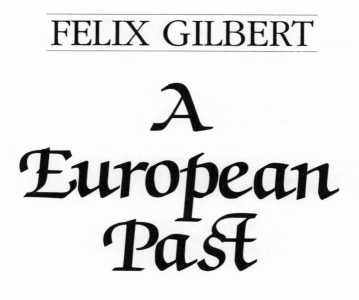

A European Past

MEMOIRS
1905   1945

W·W·NORTON & COMPANY

NEW YORK   LONDON

Copyright © 1988 by Felix Gilbert
All rights reserved.
Published simultaneously in Canada by Penguin Books Canada Ltd.,
2801 John Street, Markham, Ontario L3R 1B4.
Printed in the United States of America.

The text of this book is composed in
11.5/13.5 Garamond No. 3 Linotron 202 with a 12 pt. master,
with display type set in Zapf Chancery Demi U/LC.
Composition and manufacturing by
The Maple-Vail Book Manufacturing Group.
Book design by Margaret M. Wagner.

First Edition

Library of Congress Cataloging-in-Publication Data
Gilbert, Felix, 1905–
A European Past : memoirs, 1905–1945 / Felix Gilbert.
p. cm.
Includes index.
1. Gilbert, Felix, 1905–   .   2. Historians—Germany—
Biography.
3. Germany—History—20th century.   I. Title.
DD86.7.G5A3 1988
943'.0072024—DC19   87-25654

ISBN 0-393-02552-7

W. W. Norton & Company, Inc.
500 Fifth Avenue, New York, N. Y. 10110
W. W. Norton & Company Ltd.
37 Great Russell Street, London WC1B 3NU

1 2 3 4 5 6 7 8 9 0

To Mary

Contents

A EUROPEAN PAST

Chapter I

Summers of Childhood

IN THE AUTUMN OF 1945 I received orders to fly on a brief mission from Wiesbaden, the headquarters of the U.S. Office of Strategic Services, in which I was then serving, to Berlin. I had grown up there, and I was eager for the opportunity to see whether any traces of the past could be found in the city that had been the center of the last furious battle of the Second World War. My orders left me time to drive around in the city and to find out what had happened to the house in which my grandmother had had an apartment, and where I had lived during my years in the Gymnasium and a good part of my student days. My grandmother's apartment formed the large first floor (*Hochetage*, as the Berliners called it) of a house in a street called Tirpitz-Ufer, and was three minutes' walk from the Lützow Platz, a center of Berlin's residential quarter. Houses lined one side of the street and faced out on a row of chestnut trees bordering a canal on which, from time to time,

barges brought coal into the town. One day in the spring of
1919—I was not yet fourteen—returning from the Gymnasium, I joined a small crowd that had assembled along the
bank of the Landwehr Canal and watched a body being fished
out of the water. The men in charge of the operation told us
spectators that the body was that of Rosa Luxemburg, and
the newspapers confirmed it the next day.

I did not expect that much of this old quarter would still
be standing in 1945. Shortly before the First World War—
very near to the house of my grandmother, actually separated
only by one apartment building—the German imperial government had erected a colossal office building to serve as the
administrative headquarters of the German navy. During the
Weimar Republic, this building became the Ministry of
Defense and, under the Nazis, the seat of the OKW (Supreme
Army Command). I had no doubt that this section of Berlin
had been a prime target of air attacks.

Nevertheless, when my jeep approached the area that as a
boy I had known so well I found it unrecognizable. I did not
even know where I was. Between the canal and Berlin's central park, the Tiergarten, there had been a number of short
streets with elegant townhouses, gardens, tennis courts, and
greenhouses. The area was thick with trees, and while it was
possible to look from the windows of my grandmother's
apartment into the garden of the neighboring house, one
could not see beyond. Now, in 1945, the area between the
canal and the Tiergarten was as far as the eye could see a flat,
stony desert. The chestnut trees along the canal had disappeared. Chunks of building had rolled down toward the bank
of the canal and formed an impenetrable wall of stone and
rubble. The jeep could not even come close to the Tirpitz-
Ufer, so I asked the driver to wait at some distance while I
clambered into this field of ruins, curious to see whether there
was any sign that might indicate where the house had stood

in which I had spent, certainly with frequent absences, some twenty-five years of my life.

Suddenly I stopped. It seemed to me that if I really saw what I thought I saw, I must be dreaming. On the right side of the house in which I had lived, there had been a short cobblestone driveway leading to a broad entrance gate. Trucks and horse-drawn wagons delivering goods or removing refuse passed through this gate into the large but gloomy courtyard around which this house, like almost every other Berlin apartment house, was built. The cobblestones of the driveway formed a simple, regular pattern of white and blue: blue cobblestones in the corners, a larger cluster of blue cobblestones in the center, and a chain of blue cobblestones connecting the right corner above with the left corner below and vice versa. I was amazed to discover, among all this rubble, the pattern of these blue and white cobblestones. They called back to my mind a remote past because they had played an important role in my childhood.

To a small boy, it was an irresistible challenge to try to jump from blue cobblestone to blue cobblestone without touching or landing on one of the white cobblestones in between. But I had had little opportunity to indulge in this tempting game, because I was not permitted to play on the street. The chance came just once a year on an occasion of great importance: the move to Charlottenburg.

When I was between two and five years old, we moved every year early in May from Berlin to the more rural neighboring town of Charlottenburg. On the morning of the move, the apartment in which we lived during the winter was shut. During the days before the move trunks were packed and closed, suitcases were strapped up the evening before, and the apartment was made ready for the summer cleaning. The furniture was pushed together in the corners of the rooms so that the rugs could be taken up and cleaned, paintings were taken down from the walls, wardrobes and cupboards were locked. On the morning of departure day, we children—my sister and I—woke up early, full of excitement. There was not much else for the frantic adults and harried servants to do but send us down to the street to wait for the wagon that would take our household goods to Charlottenburg, and then to wait for the carriages in which we would follow.

It was exciting to see and hear what was going on in the street at a time when I was usually still asleep: the milk wagons, whose coming was announced by the ringing of little bells so that people could come down and fill their milk bottles from the faucets that lined the outside of the wagon, the white-clad baker boys, who carried the famous Berlin *Semmel* (a special crisp roll) in little linen bags, and the big, heavy horses that drew the wagons with barrels of beer. But these excitements passed quickly, and the more reliable entertainment was to jump from blue cobblestone to blue cobblestone until the carriages taking us to Charlottenburg finally appeared. Playing on the pattern of the driveway was the beginning of the summer in Charlottenburg.

CHARLOTTENBURG

I DOUBT that today people driving through the western part of Berlin know when they have reached the border between Berlin and Charlottenburg: To get from Lützow Platz to Charlottenburg by car does not take more than ten minutes even in rush hour, and even in the years of my youth—the first decade of the twentieth century—many Berliners probably found it ridiculous to move for the summer months from Berlin to Charlottenburg. In the nineteenth century, however, it had been the accepted custom of the well-to-do to move in the summer to the villas and gardens of Charlottenburg. But after Berlin became an imperial capital and spread out, these differences were soon effaced and there was not much point in continuing this custom.

In my family respect for the patriarch rather than observance of a tradition was the motive for continuing the habit. The villa in Charlottenburg belonged to my great-grandfather, Otto Georg Oppenheim, then in his early nineties: to him the move to Charlottenburg in the summer was an established pattern of life and, since he was a widower, an opportunity to assemble his family, or at least part of his large family, around him during the summer months.

The house in Charlottenburg was a large place. The central part was occupied by great-grandfather Oppenheim. The right wing had two apartments: the higher one was inhabited by my grandmother, Enole Mendelssohn Bartholdy, and her daughter (my mother) with us, her two children; the lower one by a younger sister of my grandmother with her three daughters. In the left wing of the house the eldest son of my great-grandfather, a banker, lived with his extensive family. The house was surrounded by a spacious garden. A few dark corners—with rhododendrons and thick bushes, large shade trees, the ground covered with the green leaves of lilies of the valley—gave occasion for a little child to imagine daring adventures. The rest was a formal garden, well planted with flower beds and paths lined with rose bushes and fuchsias, so that from the broad terrace behind the center of the house the view extended over a wide lawn.

I believe I remember my great-grandfather sitting on the terrace in front of the house in a brown velvet jacket, a black silken cap on his head and a rug over his knees. The only events of early childhood that leave a trace in your memory are those in which you played a part, and the memory I have of the old gentleman, I am sure, comes from what we did together during the Charlottenburg summers: we would regularly take a drive after the midday meal on days of good weather. The carriage stood at the front entrance with the

coachman on the box and a manservant ready to open the
door when my great-grandfather appeared. After he had settled in the carriage, I was placed next to him—always in a
white frock. (This I remember clearly because every day there
was a little fight: I protested the need for putting on a clean
frock for this occasion.) The drive was usually short and I
found everything interesting—streets, woods, the great gates
to the park of the Charlottenburg Palace, the summer residence of the Hohenzollern kings. I am afraid I was rather
proud sitting next to my great-grandfather, looking down
from the carriage on the people walking on the streets. It has
never become clear to me whether I owed the honor of accompanying my great-grandfather to my being the youngest of
his great-grandchildren, or to the fact that my great-grandfather was hard of hearing and a companion with whom he
did not need to converse seemed to him the most agreeable.

The few grown-up and older people who play a role in
one's childhood almost always remain firmly implanted in
one's memory, and the great-grandfather who took me as a
companion on his daily drives continued to remain a figure
of curiosity and authority for me even in later years. As a
young man I frequently asked my relations about him, but
the various stories I was told did not fit together, and he has
remained for me a puzzling figure. As contradictory and confusing as the stories are, they allow a glimpse into the last
century, so different and so remote despite its closeness in
time.

Great-grandfather Oppenheim came from a family of successful Jewish bankers who had made their money in Königs-
berg, East Prussia; his parents then had moved to Berlin, and
there he married a daughter of Alexander Mendelssohn, head
of the Mendelssohn banking house and grandson of Moses
Mendelssohn, the Enlightenment philosopher. Thus the later
heads of the Mendelssohn bank were my great-grandfather's
nephews, and these ties with the Mendelssohn family were

reinforced by the marriage of one of his daughters—my grandmother—to the second son of Felix Mendelssohn Bartholdy. Great-grandfather Oppenheim had two other daughters—one was the wife of a Prussian army officer, the other was married to a professor of medicine at the University of Berlin. He also had two sons; the elder one was a banker, the other studied chemistry and became the chairman of a large chemical and photographic company, the AGFA (Aktiengesellschaft für Anilinfabrikation), which had been founded by my grandfather Paul Mendelssohn Bartholdy. Briefly, great-grandfather Oppenheim was the head of a very large family with many grandchildren and great-grandchildren. Although descended from a Jewish family, he must have been baptized early in the nineteenth century when he married the daughter of Alexander Mendelssohn, because all the Mendelssohns had been baptized in the first half of the nineteenth century; moreover, he pursued a career in the Prussian judicial system which he could not have done without having been baptized.

Early in his career there was a crisis. His name does not appear in books on German nineteenth-century history, but his brother Alexander Oppenheim is sometimes mentioned. Alexander was an enthusiastic disciple of Ferdinand Lassalle, the brilliant protagonist of the workers' movement and defender of the oppressed. Lassalle got deeply involved in the affair of a Gräfin Hatzfeldt, who could not get a divorce from her husband although he had betrayed and humiliated her. To help Lassalle, Alexander Oppenheim, together with a relation from the Mendelssohn family, stole from Count Hatzfeldt a box of documents that were expected to compromise the count and to make possible the divorce the count had refused. The theft of this box of documents became a widely publicized affair. In defense of his two followers, Lassalle made one of his great speeches, but even that did not keep Alexander Oppenheim from being sent to prison; he was soon released, however, when Alexander von Humboldt, a close friend of the Mendelssohn family, intervened with the Prussian king.

Letters show that my great-grandfather was deeply shocked and upset by his brother's behavior. Strangely enough, his judicial career seems not to have suffered. As a representative of the Prussian government he was sent to Rome to buy the Palazzo Caffarelli on the Capitoline for the government, and until the First World War this palace served first as the Prussian and then as the German embassy. My great-grandfather advanced quickly in the Prussian judicial administration, and retired as a member of one of the highest Prussian law courts. It was reported in the family that after the foundation of the empire in 1871, he was offered a position on the bench of the newly created federal court in Leipzig but refused because he did not want to leave Berlin; and so he took an early retirement. I find this story somewhat suspect because stories of the great prizes that members of a family could have had but refused are all too common. It must be said, however, that he was and remained throughout his life a close friend of Heinrich von Friedberg, Bismarck's minister of justice.

All this implies a conformist and conservative outlook, and an amusing confirmation of this view was given me by my mother's youngest brother. He told me that when he was a student in his early twenties, he was once sent to discuss the arrangements for a family party with the lady who served as housekeeper-companion to my widowed great-grandfather. This lady, a dignified gentlewoman in her sixties, and my uncle withdrew to a small sitting room where they accomplished their business in less than an hour. For the next three days my great-grandfather refused to speak to his housekeeper, and when she finally asked him why he would not talk to her, he replied that he was indignant, and needed time to overcome his indignation, because she had, he explained, spent almost an hour alone with a young man.

However, I also learned of features that do not correspond

to this image of a gentleman of the upper class rigorously holding to the most old-fashioned and conservative standards of behavior. My great-grandfather seems to have felt strongly bound by the obligations of great wealth. He ordered that every beggar who appeared at the back door of his apartment on the Pariser Platz in Berlin ought to be given one mark, a goodly sum at the time. Word got around, of course, and the beggars queued up at the door until the police intervened and suggested that other methods of supporting poor people would be more appropriate.

Whether my great-grandfather's attitude to the poor revealed his roots in a preindustrial world or whether it was an expression of a social conscience is difficult to say. The striking and strange fact is that politically this strict and correct Prussian civil servant was a liberal. To the end of his life he voted for the Progressive People's Party, the left wing of the Liberals, the bourgeois party nearest to the Socialists. And after his retirement he devoted himself to translating the foremost English textbook on parliamentary procedure into German. He abhorred the luxury and the ostentatiousness of Germany under William II, and for several months he refused to see his grandson, Otto Mendelssohn Bartholdy, the eldest brother of my mother, because Otto had paid a price—in likelihood a hefty contribution to the building of a church in Berlin in memory of Kaiser William—in return for being ennobled by William II.

The figure of this great-grandfather, although by no means a person of historical importance, seems to me worth delineating. This strange combination of correctness and independence was probably feasible only in the liberal nineteenth century; today we are much more aware of the class structure of the society in which we live, and of the extent to which our outlook and our behavior are determined by the class to which we belong. We recognize a close interrelationship between political concerns and social attitudes. But these reflections came to me only when I developed my interest in history, which I needed in order to understand the gentleman-patriarch who had been a dominant figure in my early years.

My personal memories of the house, the garden, the summer life in Charlottenburg, are vague. Two episodes have remained with me and I suspect left traces in my life. One summer in Charlottenburg I had scarlet fever and had to spend most of the time in bed, closed off from the world, with the exception of a nurse who took care of me, and the daily visits of my mother. In the course of the four or six weeks I gradually assembled most of my toys on my bed, or at least in the room to which I was confined. I was told that everything I touched might be contaminated and would have to be burned. (I find it difficult to understand why it was considered necessary to give me this information, but the fact is firm in my mind.) Finally my quarantine was over and I was allowed to rejoin my relations and playmates. They were in a room behind high, wide folding doors that I could open only by raising myself on the tips of my toes to reach the door latch. With great effort I opened the doors, and there, in front of me on the floor, were all the toys with which I had played during my illness; I had eyes for nothing else. I was overwhelmed by the surprise and pleasure of again having the toys I believed had been destroyed. For the first time in my highly organized and strictly regulated childhood I had an experience that I would have many times in the future but that, at its first occurrence, was upsetting as well as exciting: that unexpected things happen in life, that one never knows what will happen.

One other day in Charlottenburg had the same lasting impact. My great-grandfather had died and the house was sold. The distribution and removal of the furniture kept the family busy for many weeks. Finally we were taken to Charlottenburg to have a last look at the house. I remember that my sister and I were sitting on the floor of a big empty room, looking through a long, flat, hemispherical window that rounded off a large window of a hall on the lower floor. It gave a broad, rather extended view of the courtyard. The furniture vans were loaded, the horses led out of the stables, the carriages removed. Even at this time of childhood I became aware that one could not always have things remain as they had been before, that there is an end to everything. I believe it was October, and the leaves were falling; but I may be imagining that. Perhaps it was not the season but the atmosphere of this last visit to Charlottenburg which was that of autumn.

THE SALZKAMMERGUT

FOR a number of years after the house in Charlottenburg had been sold, we spent our summers—the months of July and August—in Rindbach, a small village at the southern end of the Traunsee in the Austrian Salzkammergut. Each year we stayed in the same house, which was situated along the main village street; for the peasant owners, who moved during our stay to live with neighbors, our coming provided a regular addition to their income. What they did with their own belongings I will never know. They left ample space for us, and the rooms were soon filled with the furniture, curtains, and tablecloths my mother and grand-mother had acquired or brought from Berlin.

My bedroom was on the second floor. On clear and cool nights, when I was supposed to be in bed and asleep, I would get up to look out of the window. Straight ahead, I saw a large meadow ascending gradually into a line of hills. The hills were overtopped by a chain of mountains and between and above two of these mountains rose the snow-covered peak of the Dachstein, standing out in blinding whiteness from the black mountains and the dark sky.

When I looked down from my window, I saw a corner of the small garden that surrounded our house. Almost hiding the wooden fence that enclosed the garden stood a row of colorful phlox, which, from the flickering light of large candles and an oil lamp, gave off a faint pinkish glow. The lamp and candles, placed in glass tubes as protection against the wind, stood on a table around which my mother and grandmother and some of their friends sat talking and doing needlework; the silken neckerchiefs that the ladies, following native custom, were wearing added yet more color. I didn't understand their words, but the murmuring reached up to my window and assured me of the presence of human society. The permanence of the mountains and the steady sounds of human company radiated a tranquillity that kept away the fears which the darkness of the night might arouse. But this tranquillity was created without my having anything to do with it, or being asked to do anything. My feelings of security and remoteness were closely tied together.

Without impeding the enjoyment of what I saw and did, this feeling of remoteness formed the undertone of my summers in Austria. It was nourished by a variety of experiences. First of all, each summer there was the need to change my external appearance in acceptance of native custom. Recently I found two photographs of myself as a child, one taken in Berlin, the other in the Salzkammergut. In Berlin I am wearing a large, wheel-like Panama hat on my head. The hat must have covered my back down to my hips. I was extremely proud of this hat. When on a trip to Austria we stopped in Munich and visited the Frauenkirche, I marched proudly into the church with the Panama hat on my head; after a few minutes a young priest appeared, shouted at me angrily, and tore my beloved Panama hat from my head. I was near crying, but before the tears started the priest was persuaded that, coming from north Germany, I did not realize what I had been doing by keeping a hat on my head in church, and he released the hat. But this frightening event on my first visit to the Frauenkirche has thrown no shadow on my love for this church; no visit to Munich, not even one of only a few hours, seems right to me without a visit to the Frauenkirche.

After this incident in the Frauenkirche I must have abandoned my Panama hat quickly because we arrived in Rindbach later that day, and the photograph taken there shows me as a native of the region, with leather breeches and a Tyrolean hat. I soon became an expert on leather breeches, full of contempt for imitations that were not, like mine, of soft, genuine gray leather. I also wore suspenders that were of green leather and embroidered with Alpine flowers. If I had no difficulty in appearing in Tyrolean clothes, I found it much more difficult to go barefoot, as most of the children in the village did. The village street of muddy clay was interlaced on the right and left by stripes of small, sharp stones which kept carriages from getting stuck in the mud after the frequent rains. To cross the street one had to take a few steps on these stony stripes, and since I was unused to going barefoot, the stones were painful to my tender soles. This was a tragedy because four houses distant, on the other side of the street, lived my first great love, the daughter of a Viennese family who spent a good part of the year in Rindbach. It was always a hard decision to undergo the pain of crossing the street, and when I was at her place we frequently decided to walk into the woods at the end of the village. I made a rather miserable figure limping behind her and her brother, who did not understand what made me linger.

Language also formed an obstacle to sociability. I found it impossible to understand the villagers—young and old—and my Viennese cousins (a sister of my mother had married an Austrian and lived in Vienna) were inclined to ridicule my north German. They could not hide their amusement when I

used for "piece of string" the German word *Bindfaden,* and
not the Austrian *Spakat.* In Rindbach the superiority of my
cousins was undeniable. One had a great gift for taming pretty
mountain squirrels; he usually carried a squirrel in his sleeve.
The other was most adept at hitting thieving birds with his
sling, whereas I could never hit anything. The most humili-
ating moment came on the exciting occasion when my grandmother decided to rent a car. We were discussing what the
color of this car ought to be. I was for a red car, my cousins
voted for blue, and when the car arrived it was blue. This
defeat left me with anti-Austrian feelings which took me a
long time to overcome.

There was a more cogent reason why this feeling of
remoteness colored my life in Rindbach. The place was not a
tourist resort. It had no hotel or inn, and the number of
summer visitors was small. It was a village of peasants who
made some additional money by renting their houses in the
summer months. A few families from Vienna had their houses
there and came every summer. The small group of summer
visitors had little contact with Rindbach's permanent residents and formed their own little world in which everyone
knew everybody else. In contrast to Berlin, where at any time
I might have encountered people I did not know and felt
anxious because I did not know what was expected from me,
in Rindbach I moved only among people whom I knew and
who knew me. I felt I had a secure place. The feelings of
security and remoteness that suffused the view I had at night
from my bedroom window characterized my entire existence
in Rindbach.

The summer residents were a colony, but a colony of a
particular character: a music colony. We went to Rindbach
because Franz von Mendelssohn, a cousin of my grandmother, one of the chiefs of the Mendelssohn bank in Berlin,
had built his own house there on a hillock slightly above the
village. He was very musical, and his house contained a large

room suited for music making. He persuaded several well-known musicians to join him in Rindbach during the summer. The most exciting figure among them was the pianist Artur Schnabel, who always seemed to enjoy both amusing and frightening us youngsters. There were other distinguished musicians, like Carl Flesch, professor of violin at the Berlin Academy for Music, and various singers such as Schnabel's wife, and the then famous Jeannette de Jong. As is well known, it rains a lot in the Salzkammergut, and on rainy days, music—and very good music—was made. I cannot say, however, that I found this particularly entertaining—partly because I am not a musician and not especially musical, and partly because as a small boy I had to sit on the floor in front of the first row of chairs. I was directly under the eye of the musicians in front of me and of the adults behind me; all could notice whether I behaved well and was sitting still.

Jeannette de Jong's husband, who probably heard enough music in his own home, shared my feelings. Several times when these concerts threatened to take place he escaped them by asking me to play chess with him. I played chess rather well at a very young age but my chess career ended ten years later when my mother, worried by my absorption in the game, promised me one mark for every week in which I did not touch a chess board. During the years in Rindbach, however, I was grateful for any opportunity to show my expertise in chess, and when asked to play I would walk proudly along the village street with the board and the box of chess pieces under my arm.

While teaching at Bryn Mawr College after the Second World War, I regularly offered a course called "European History from 1890 to the Present." In one of the first meetings of the class I liked to remark that as a young boy I had presented flowers to Emperor Francis Joseph of Austria-Hungary. It was a very simple event. The Austrian emperor, who spent his summers in Ischl—a famous resort not far from

Rindbach—would stop in our village to change from his large carriage into a dog cart, which could carry him up into the mountains to hunt chamois around the Traunsee. The change of vehicles took place on a small square in front of the Rindbach post office, where grown-ups and children assembled to see the emperor. Once or twice I was chosen to give the emperor a bunch of flowers, probably for no other reason than that I was the right age and that the postmaster, who made the selection, might have found me somewhat cleaner than the peasant children. As far as I remember, there was little to this event. The old gentleman bowed and took the flowers, but I don't even remember whether he said thank you.

Whenever I told the story of my encounter with the emperor Francis Joseph to my Bryn Mawr students, their reaction was highly amusing. At first they seemed to think that the story could not be true. Then they began to speculate that I concealed my age very well, that I was much older than I seemed—almost a prehistoric figure! Only very slowly did they draw the conclusion I wanted: that the period before the First World War, the early twentieth century, still reached into their lives.

With the passing of years, however, I am inclined not only to understand the students' first reaction, but to share it. Vacationing in a small, remote village of prewar Austria certainly had its small inconveniences and little humiliations, but what you saw and encountered also possessed a certain excitement and uniqueness that now makes it seem not only a different land, but a different world.

No cakes have ever been like the cakes the Czech cook made for our Sunday dinners. The coffee mélange, the sweets and tarts you ate in the *Konditorei* (café) in Gmunden, which you reached after a trip on the steamer over the entire Traunsee, have never been equaled. Although I have been on higher and more spectacular mountains, none since has given the satisfaction I had when, climbing up the stony beds of waterfalls, I reached the pasture above the tree line and drank the fresh milk from the cows grazing there.

That alien world into which I was plunged during the summer months not only developed in me a sense of remoteness and unreality; it also brought me into immediate contact with phenomena that I had previously known only as spectacles or through hearsay, but that I now experienced in their strength and power.

One night a babble of voices and a certain unrest awakened me. I was told to look out of the window, and I saw, at some distance, on the border of the woods, a house burning. I could clearly see the flames rising, dancing in and out of the windows, against the background of dark woods and dark sky. And then I saw the walls collapse. Because the house was secluded, the few firemen of the village could do little, and all that remained was a ruin. When we visited the scene the next day, the peasant owners of the house were sitting on some furniture they had saved, and they accepted with gratitude the food and clothes that we brought to them.

Dramatic changes on the Traunsee also taught me about forces that could not be controlled. Blue-black clouds would suddenly arise behind the rocky peaks of the surrounding mountains, and in a few minutes the lake would be transformed into a boiling caldron. Proof of the dangerous powers of the storm was a small, picturesque cemetery on a peninsula reaching out into the lake. In one corner of the cemetery were something like thirty simple wooden crosses, each with a small white plate in the center inscribed with a name, date of birth, and date of death. The date of death was always the same. All had been together in a boat that had capsized in one of these storms. Although I have seen many shocking and depressing mass burial sites since, this small cemetery uniting grandmothers and grandchildren, brothers and sisters, relations and friends, all dead the same day, remains in my mind as a reminder of life's fragility.

NORDWIJK

MY MOTHER, my sister, and I spent the month of July 1914 in Nordwijk—a sea resort on the Dutch coast. Our stay there was very different from the summers in Charlottenburg and Rindbach: it was unique, not a recurring event. By this time I had passed my ninth birthday and was no longer a small child. I was attending the Gymnasium in Berlin and beginning to learn Latin. Since I had shown some interest in political events, I was permitted to read the first page of the newspaper, which contained the political news, and the inside pages with the sports news. However, I soon discovered that the inside pages also contained a novel appearing in serialized form. One of my worries about the trip to Nordwijk was that I might never know how this novel would turn out. It was *Jettchen Gebert* by Georg Herrmann, a story about Berlin in the middle of the nineteenth century, and much of it took place in Charlottenburg, where the characters in the novel moved for the summer. I must have been able to get hold of the newspaper even in Nordwijk because I remember that I was saddened by the story's tragic end.

We did not settle in Nordwijk for several months with a household of our own as we had in Rindbach, but we were there as tourists for a few weeks and stayed in a hotel—Huis ter Duin—which I have been told still exists. It was built above the dunes, and from the windows of the dining room there was a magnificent view of the North Sea. I spent mornings on the beach building sand castles and wading in the sea as far as I could go until the waves knocked me down. In the afternoons I played tennis on a court built among the dunes; actually I spent most of the afternoon looking in the dunes for tennis balls I had hit so high and wide that they had landed outside the court. A cousin of my mother also spent the summer vacation in Nordwijk, and we all made excursions by car to the towns of the interior—Leiden and Utrecht.

After the Frauenkirche in Munich, St. Stephen's in Vienna, and the village churches of the Salzkammergut with their painted walls and altars full of colorful and gilded wood-carved figures, I found the bleak black-and-white interior of the churches in the Netherlands cold and disappointing.

Although being a tourist in Nordwijk was very different from the settled life in Charlottenburg and the Salzkammergut, the summers I spent in these three places belong together for me. All three were permeated by an atmosphere of security and permanence. Though this might not have seemed the best possible world, there was a definite place in it for me and my family, and I thought this world would go on forever as it was. The First World War swept all this away—both this world and my feelings about it—and although the disappearance of what might be called my arrogant complacency might be a good thing, that disappearance establishes for me a sharp dividing line between the period before 1914 and after, and endows the world before 1914 with the tinge of a golden fairy tale.

My feeling that the summer in Nordwijk was the last moment of a life that would not return was not a feeling of which I have become gradually aware over the course of years; it had its roots in the abruptness and excitement with which we broke off our stay in Nordwijk—two weeks earlier than had been planned. Mr. Ernst von Simson, the husband of my mother's cousin, was a high civil servant in the imperial German government, and was aware of the crisis that was brewing. Before leaving Berlin for Nordwijk toward the end of July, he had arranged that if war seemed likely, his office was to send him a telegram that, although harmless in its wording, would warn us to return to Germany. The telegram arrived, and on the same day (I think it was July 28) we packed our belongings in great haste and took the first train back to Germany. Friends and acquaintances, unaware of the special source of the warning we had received, considered us

unnecessarily frightened. I recall a gentleman saying to my
mother at the railroad station: "It is all nonsense. You will
be back here in a week."

I was young, and the excitement of the sudden departure
and the expectation of what lay ahead—the train ride and a
stay in the house of an uncle, since our Berlin apartment was
closed—compensated for the premature end of the vacation.
I regretted leaving Nordwijk mainly for one reason: each
morning, at breakfast at the Huis ter Duin, a basket of soft,
round buns with sweet raisins in them was put on our table.
They were a perfect delight, and have remained for me the
symbol of a time when the world was at peace.

After returning from the Netherlands to Germany (which
I believe was the last time I crossed a European frontier without passport or any boundary control), we went to Potsdam
for a week until our apartment in Berlin was opened and the
servants had returned. In Potsdam we stayed in the house of
my mother's eldest brother, Otto von Mendelssohn Bartholdy, who had been a banker but had retired when he was
still quite young. Although he remained on the board of several companies, he had left Berlin and the world of business
and lived in Potsdam. He was somewhat distant from the
rest of the family, but when I went to study in Heidelberg
at the height of the German inflation in 1923, he called me
to his office, gave me a bank note, and told me I should try
to have a good time. When I later looked at the bank note, I
discovered that it was an American fifty-dollar bill. I lived
on this money my entire first semester—almost four months—
traveled during the rest of that summer, and still had ten
dollars left in the fall when the German currency was stabilized.

My uncle's house, situated somewhat outside Potsdam on
one of the many lakes around the town, resembled an English
country house. It was surrounded by a large garden, which
in front rolled gracefully down to the lake. In the back the

garden rose gently to a small hill from which there was a broad view of the lake, and of the fields and woods on the other side of the lake. In the late afternoon on one of the first days after our return from Nordwijk, we—my mother, my aunt and uncle, my sister, and I—walked up the hill at the end of the garden to view the sunset. I remember my aunt saying: "The sun sets red; there will be war."

On this hill, quite close to the spot where my aunt spoke her prophetic words, stood a gardener's cottage, and that was where my uncle was living when I returned to Berlin in 1945. The Nazis had forced him out of his big house, and he had then lived in an apartment over the stables; when the Russians came he was forced to leave this apartment, and he had moved to the gardener's cottage. In Berlin I had heard that he was still living in Potsdam. I was eager to see him, and so it came to what proved to be our last meeting. American relations with the Russians were still amicable in 1945; I had no difficulty driving into the Russian zone, and easily found my way to my uncle's place. The cottage had three very small rooms, which he shared with two other people. The largest room, which seemed to be his, had some good furniture from the main house and some cheap, fragile pieces that looked as though they had been gathered from a bombed house.

My uncle was enormously pleased that I had managed to get to him. When I made some remark about the harshness of the conditions in which he now lived, he said that he did not mind; the main thing was that the Nazi regime had ended and that the war was over. After something like an hour I said that it seemed time for me to get back to my billet in Berlin. At this mention of the passing of time my uncle commented that almost the only thing he found difficult to bear was that he never knew what time it was, because the Russians had taken everyone's watches and all the clocks. My instinctive reaction to his remark was to take my watch off my wrist and give it to him, but alas my watch had stopped

just before I had left Wiesbaden for Berlin, and an OSS colleague had loaned me his gold watch at the last moment. Of
course I could not give away a watch that was not mine; or
should I have? The question still bothers me.

Chapter II

Why
I Became a
Historian

WHY DID I become a historian? My brief answer is that the first book I was able to read by myself was a history book, a collection of historical biographies called *Grube's Geschichtsbilder*. After finishing the book I said to my mother: "I want to become a professor of history." The story is true, and I enjoy giving this simple answer instead of the more complicated story that is the subject of this chapter.

I certainly did not pursue the aim of becoming a professor of history as constantly and single-mindedly as my brief answer might suggest. There was a time when I wanted to become a painter. There were enough musicians and artists among the members of the Mendelssohn family and among our friends to make this a thoroughly respectable and acceptable choice. However, because these artists—from Joseph Joachim to Artur Schnabel, from Anton von Werner to Max Liebermann—were recognized as outstanding, the standards of judgement in my family were high, and I was told early that you should enter upon such a career only when you had quite unusual gifts. Fortunately I soon became aware that my talent for drawing and painting could hardly be considered an unusual gift, and my abandonment of this plan was received by my relations with a sigh of relief.

I then played with the idea of studying philosophy. During my last two school years a cousin of mine, Joachim Wach, was studying philosophy in Berlin and we became good friends. His example drew me toward the field, but my mother actively opposed this. She told me: "When you are in Heidelberg, you can attend what courses or lectures you want, but don't say that you study philosophy. All philosophers are crazy." Generalizations are doubtful, and the remark shows only that philosophers in Germany were believed to live in an unreal world.

In my first semester at Heidelberg I decided quickly and assuredly to make history my principal field of study. The reason, of course, was not that history was the subject of the first book I had read, nor that other plans did not work out. The study of history seemed to me of overwhelming importance and irresistible attraction because of the world in which I had grown up, a world of politics. I was nine and had just entered the Gymnasium when the First World War broke out; I was thirteen when the war ended in defeat and Germany became a republic; I was eighteen and had just completed my first semester at the University of Heidelberg when the German inflation led to near civil war in Saxony and Bavaria and to the devaluation of the mark. War, revolution, and social turmoil, in an interlocking chain, shaped the crucial years of my youth.

Too young to fight in the war, but old enough to have to decide about my future course before the world had again settled into a stable pattern, I felt—and many of my contemporaries shared this feeling—that we belonged to a special

generation, different from the ones that preceded and followed mine. Skeptical about the values of the past, we were
also skeptical about the likelihood of stability in the future.

When I began to study history, it was mainly, almost
exclusively, political history. I assumed, therefore, that an
understanding of politics could be acquired only—or mainly—
from history. But if my interest in history is not difficult to
explain, I have frequently wondered why, almost from the
outset, my political views have had what might be called a
left-wing character. Proof of this were the lively disputes I
had with my friend Hans-Werner von Brandenstein during
the last years of the war, while we were still in our early
teens. His father was a great landowner in Mecklenburg, an
East Elbian Junker. The Brandensteins were an extremely
conservative family. They lived in Berlin during the war years
because the father was the representative of the grand duke
of Mecklenburg on the German Federal Council. On the way
to and from our school—a walk of almost thirty minutes
through the Tiergarten—Hans-Werner and I had the most
vehement political debates; we passionately discussed all the
questions that excited public opinion.

One of the focal points of our disputes was the so-called
Peace Resolution of the German Reichstag of 1917, which
advocated a peace without annexations and which I heartily
approved of and Hans-Werner attacked. Another issue was
the question of submarine warfare: whether Germany should
keep within the recognized boundaries of sea warfare or proceed unrestrictedly. I fear that my opposition to unrestricted
submarine warfare was less determined by concern for the
maintenance of international law than by the view that unrestricted submarine warfare would not have the effect of forcing England to surrender. Hans-Werner, of course, was in
favor of unrestricted submarine warfare, and one morning on
the way to school he reported triumphantly that his father
had told him, under the vow of silence, that a declaration of

unrestricted submarine warfare would be made; it became
public the next day.

Our differences were strongest, however, about two questions of internal policy. I was in favor of liberalizing the Prussian voting system, which Emperor William II in an Easter
message of 1917 had promised in order to stimulate the flag-
ging war enthusiasm. And I also approved of the parliamen-
tarization of the government, which took place in the late
summer of 1918. Hans-Werner was vehemently opposed to
both these measures. These differences did no harm to our
friendship, however, and I regretted very much that after the
revolution the Brandensteins left Berlin for their estates in
Mecklenburg.

In thinking back to these years of the First World War, I
find it quite surprising that I had such pronounced political
views. They were not prescribed to me, and though family
influences played some role, I suspect that the war produced
in me a change from enthusiasm to disillusionment, and that
this change was decisive in patterning my political outlook.

WAR

I WAS nine years old when the war broke out, and I reacted
as did most boys at this age: with patriotic excitement and
enthusiasm for our soldiers and generals. After the announce-
ment of a German victory—and they were frequent in the
first months of the war—I walked with some companions to
the great square before the Imperial Palace, sang patriotic
songs with the assembled crowd, and called for the appearance of the emperor or some member of the royal house. In
the afternoons after school was over, my friends and I played
soldiers in the garden of our apartment house. When the
weather was bad and I had to be inside, I carved little wooden
ships that approximated the ships of the German navy as they

appeared in photographs in the navy yearbook. I also played with tin soldiers, and a table in my room was always filled with tin soldiers organized in battle order. I am a living refutation of the thesis that playing with soldiers makes you militarily- and war-minded. Until the Nazis came to power I was a pacifist. On the other hand, from these early years on, I have maintained a lively interest in military institutions and military affairs. Understanding the role of the army in the social structure and its influence on policy-making seems to me a prerequisite for understanding the strength and weaknesses of a political order.

In the early years of the war I worshiped everyone in uniform. I remember the immense pride with which I accompanied my Austrian cousin when, during his leave, he visited my grandmother in Berlin. He was a good-looking young officer in an elite Austrian regiment, the Tiroler Kaiserjäger, whose uniform was light blue and silver. To my delight everyone looked admiringly at him when we walked through the streets of Berlin. I was among the family members who took him to his train when he returned to his regiment. The other Austrian officers who were traveling on the same train introduced themselves to each other, and immediately began to address each other by the intimate *du*. Used to the stiff and distant attitude of Prussian officers, I was highly astonished at this, almost shocked. As in the summers in Rindbach, I was made aware of the deep-rooted differences even among people who speak the same language.

The degree to which life preserved its prewar pattern, at least during the first two or three years of the war, seems to me most surprising. While my father was still alive my parents had lived in Baden-Baden, where my father, a physician, was the director of a sanatorium. My father died when I was nine months old, and my mother moved back to Berlin to live with her mother. But she had many friends in Baden-Baden, and each spring we spent a short vacation there; we continued these visits even during the war. Some of the great luxury hotels were closed or transformed into hospitals, and the visitors strolling along the famous Lichtenthaler Avenue might have been fewer and less elegant than in peacetime. Occasionally you heard the rumble of guns firing on the other side of the Rhine. And once or twice some excitement was caused by a French airplane flying over the town, although at that time there was no fear that it would drop bombs. But for many, vacations in Baden-Baden in wartime were not very different from what they had been in peacetime.

The two world wars are frequently seen as links in a chain, the Second World War reproducing the horrors of the first on a widened scale. In the First World War, however, life inside Germany basically continued on its previous course; the war brought about no intermingling of social classes, no regrouping of the social hierarchy. Thus, after the First World War the forces that had dominated Germany in the prewar period were still strong, and they made their weight felt in foreign and domestic policy. The thoroughness of the destruction that took place after the Second World War created unimaginable misery, but it had the one virtue of forcing Germany to rebuild from the ground up.

Although life in Germany mainly continued on its ordinary course during the First World War, I don't want to imply that we were not constantly aware of living in wartime. At the Gymnasium the war was certainly ever present. After what were regarded as decisive German military victories—the defeat of the Russians in Galicia or the battle against the English fleet at Skagerrak—we were assembled in the auditorium, and after some patriotic speeches and songs we were given a holiday. We knew that enrollment in the two highest grades was very low because many of those who had reached these grades had volunteered for the army and were away in the war. From time to time news reached us that one or another of them had been killed.

We younger boys in the Gymnasium were organized to collect war loans and to shovel snow in wintertime. I—and most of my contemporaries—found these activities disagreeable as well as unnecessary. Money for war loans was collected, if I remember correctly, as soon as a new series of loans was issued, which meant almost every six months. A street of apartment houses, usually in a rather poor district, was assigned to us, and proceeding in pairs we rang the bell of every apartment in the house. We asked for a small amount of money—I believe two marks was the smallest, twenty marks the largest amount we were entitled to receive—and we handed over to the contributor a receipt that could be cashed with interest when the war loan was repaid. Actually, things never went as smoothly as that. Usually the doors were closed before our noses as soon as we had explained what we were doing, but even friendly receptions did not automatically result in contributions. In order not to appear lazy or unpatriotic at school the next day, when contributions were to be handed in, I appeared with money I had collected from family members, and I know that many of my comrades did the same.

Snow shoveling was still more senseless, though of course it was true that because of the war the manpower needed to remove snow and ice from Berlin's wintry streets was not available. Thus we were ordered to meet at school one hour before the regular beginning of classes, shovels and picks were handed out to us, and we were sent to a nearby corner where we were expected to clean the streets of snow. These wintry mornings in Berlin could be unbelievably cold. Shivering and miserable with cold, we hacked into the frozen snow and perhaps had cleared two yards when an hour had passed, school was beginning, and we were expected to assemble in the classroom. We were old enough and intelligent enough to realize that collecting money for war loans and an hour of snow shoveling were futile enterprises; we grumbled a lot but were also proud that we were doing some kind of war service.

And these activities certainly did not extinguish our patriotic
enthusiasm.

The greatest hardship—as is well known—for people living in German cities during the war was the lack of food,
which became very noticeable during the winters of 1916–
17 and 1917–18. I abhorred the bread we had to eat: it was
very heavy, very dark and contained what I can describe only
as pieces of wood. Every morning I received two slices of this
bread and between them some tasteless paste. I was to take
them to school and eat them there during recesses. Consequently I was confronted by a most unpleasant dilemma. I
could not eat this bread because it nauseated me, yet I could
not throw it away in school because, if discovered, my behavior would be regarded as highly unpatriotic. I could not take
it home because this would have worried my mother; I was
very thin and she believed that I ought to eat more. My
solution to this dilemma was to throw the bread into the
Spree. Our house, and the Tiergarten through which I went
to school, were on one side of the river Spree, and the Gymnasium I attended was on the other side, directly behind a
broad bridge. The railing of the bridge consisted of a series
of closely placed iron bars. If I kept quite near the railing, I
could surreptitiously take the bread out of my coat pocket
and drop it between two of the iron bars into the water. My
main fear was that the sea gulls might fight for the pieces of
bread and call attention to what I was doing, but this fear
was unjustified: even the sea gulls realized that the bread was
unpalatable.

Yet, as I've said, inconveniences were no decisive reason
for becoming increasingly critical of the policy of the imperial government in the later years of the war. On the other
hand, German chauvinism did not fit the surroundings in
which I grew up. We had relations in England and personal
contacts in other countries. Knowledge of foreign languages
was considered a matter of course. We had an English gov-

erness—although only for a short time; she left a few months before the start of the war because, as my mother said, the governess was learning German very well but the children were learning no English. The unfortunate consequence of this for me was that although I could read English, I began to learn to speak it only after 1933. Though our English lessons ended when the war broke out, we continued to have French lessons twice a week at home. The lady who taught us said she was Swiss; she turned out to be a spy, unlikely as it may seem, and I thereupon declared with great energy that learning foreign languages in wartime was unpatriotic and inappropriate. My mother did not accept this argument, and two afternoons every week she spoke French and read French books with me. I suppose I was somewhat immunized against exaggerated nationalism.

An episode that occurred in the earlier years of the war contributed to my gradually developing my own opinions and not accepting all that school and official pronouncements told me about the war. At school we had to learn what I now regard as a terrible poem, "Song of Hatred Against England." One evening at home, before my grandmother, my mother, and an uncle, I recited this poem with great vigor and enthusiasm. The reception I got was remarkably cool, and I was told later by my mother that one should not indulge in hatred against people. Moreover, I should not forget that originally my father's family was English.

It seems to me probable that the rejection of chauvinism that I encountered at home instilled in me early doubts about official pronouncements and propaganda. But I must add one event of the last months of the war that was crucial in disillusioning me. It was not an event about which much can be reported. It happened at a Berlin railroad station—either the Anhalter or the Potsdamer station. We stood under the iron and glass roof which covered the railroad station and looked out along the railroad tracks that seemed to have no end. We

were there to say good-bye to my cousin, the son of my
mother's eldest brother. He had been in the army from the
beginning of the war and had participated in the battles of
the autumn of 1914, in which regiments of young volunteers
trying to reach the coastal ports of France were repulsed with
terrible losses. My cousin's regiment was so decimated that
in the following years it was employed on quieter fronts, in
the Balkans and in Turkey. But in the emergency situation
of the late summer of 1918, the regiment was ordered back
to the western front; on his way to France my cousin had had
a few days of leave in Berlin. I cannot remember that he said
anything while we stood on the platform in front of his railroad carriage. He looked terribly unhappy and depressed, and
hesitated to board the train. He did so only when the train
was almost moving. However, to a boy of thirteen who had
expected that a young officer would proudly go to the front,
the impression was crushing. It was a last step in completing
my disillusionment.

REVOLUTION

AROUND the same time, clearly influenced by the grim situation of which my cousin's behavior had made me very much
aware, I began to keep a diary; it was the only time that I
have kept a diary, and I persisted only for two or three months.
Several years later I read what I had written and disliked its
pompous tone so much that I threw the diary away. However, because I don't want to leave the impression that my
doubts and criticisms of the policy of the imperial German
government had developed into anything like a radical opposition or rejection of national values, I must confess that I do
remember very well that some of the entries from November

1918 indulged in sad and sentimental reflections about the end of Germany's imperial traditions and dreams.

My decision to keep a diary in these weeks and months shows that we lived in expectation of great changes. The events of November 1918—that is, the revolution—were neither unexpected nor surprising.

In my recollection of November 9—the day the republic was proclaimed—personal and public matters are strangely mixed. Some weeks earlier the family had been informed that one of my mother's three brothers, who had served as an officer in the army since the beginning of the war, had been killed on the eastern front. He was not killed "in action" (the war against Russia had ended), but, if I remember correctly, his death had resulted from an attempt to restore order after serious unrest had developed among the soldiers of various nationalities who were part of the German eastern army. Someone had packed together his uniform, a few books, his linen—part of which was bloody from the wound he had received—and sent them to his widow. They had lived in Leipzig, and after the news of her husband's death my aunt, Edith Mendelssohn Bartholdy, had come to Berlin to stay with my grandmother. The trunk with my uncle's belongings arrived in the apartment in Berlin on November 8, and my aunt decided to open the trunk the next morning. Understandably, she felt unable to undertake this task alone, and called me into her room to help her. It was a nightmarish experience. I knew I could help best by being cool and businesslike, but at the same time I was terribly upset. The hours I spent listing and repacking the contents of this trunk seemed longer than an entire day. However, in the midst of this, something made me aware of what was going on in the outside world. In the early afternoon I heard some noise, and leaned out the window to find out what was going on. People were rushing toward the neighboring building, which as I mentioned earlier, was the headquarters of the German navy. The commotion continued, and after a while a big red flag was hoisted over the main entrance of the navy building. The revolution had taken over.

Strangely enough, our daily routine went on as it had before. The schools were not closed, and I went to the Gymnasium every day. Relations and family friends who were civil servants, or who worked in banks or industrial enterprises, went to their offices as usual. During these weeks one event involving my mother seems to me a characteristic example of both the persistence of the old social structure and the rifts that had divided the German ruling group. When my parents lived in Baden-Baden they had been in contact with the grand ducal couple. The grand duchess, who was a daughter of the emperor William I and therefore an aunt of the emperor William II, used to visit Berlin quite regularly for a few weeks at the beginning of the winter. Having moved to Berlin after my father's death, my mother would in early winter contact one of the ladies-in-waiting of the grand duchess, who would then invite my mother for lunch or tea. Somewhat surprisingly, not even the revolution prevented the grand duchess from making her annual visit to Berlin, and staying in one of the palaces in the center of town. My mother was highly disturbed by the dilemma she now faced. She imagined that it would be extremely painful to talk with the grand duchess about the revolutionary events of the recent weeks, but the subject could hardly be entirely avoided. On the other hand, it seemed to my mother disloyal if she should not try to see the grand duchess this year. After some hesitation, she got in touch with the lady-in-waiting and was asked to come to tea. My mother told me afterward that, somewhat circumspectly, she had broached the subject of the revolution, and the grand duchess had said immediately: "Could anyone expect that the policy of this terrible nephew of mine would have had any other outcome?" (I cannot guarantee this exact wording, but it certainly corresponds to the meaning of the sentence my mother reported to me.)

Whatever its historical value, this story illustrates how traditional social patterns survived despite the "German Revolution." Princes and grand duchesses, palaces in which royalty lived, ladies-in-waiting—all continued to exist. There were traces of change under the accustomed surface, however. On several occasions I was among the onlookers when regiments returning to Berlin to be demobilized were received in a solemn ceremony on the square before the Brandenburger Tor; it was a sign of the times that they were addressed not only by an officer but also by a representative of the republican government the revolution had brought to power, i.e., the government of People's Commissars. The revolution also entered our Gymnasium: we schoolboys tried to form a school community in which not only the teachers but also the students would have something to say. In an assembly of the entire school we elected a committee in which each grade had two representatives, and this committee was to negotiate with the director about improvements in teaching and in school life that seemed to us students desirable. Considering the strict discipline that ruled a Prussian Gymnasium, this was a drastic innovation. But I must confess that after two or three months these assemblies were abandoned—probably because of clever delaying tactics by the director and his staff. Nothing more was heard of them.

The time when I became really aware that a revolution had taken place was on Christmas Eve 1918. Traditionally in the early afternoon of this day we visited the cemetery, situated somewhat south of the center of town, and from there we went to service in the Neue Kirche—not a new church, having been built in the eighteenth century, but called "new" because another, older church stood on the same square. We attended services there because, when the family had lived in the center of town, this had been their church.

On December 24, 1918, when, after the visit to the cemetery, our cab moved up the broad avenue toward the center of town, crowds were moving on both sides of the street in the same direction. Their goal was a huge building in which *Vorwärts,* the newspaper of the Socialist Party, was printed. Noise and shouting increased, and suddenly shots were fired; police appeared and a struggle took place. We were still far enough away from the church to be able to turn around and get home. We had not yet heard that on this same morning Friedrich Ebert, the leading man among the People's Commissars, had ordered an attack on the radical revolutionary sailors. They were established in a building behind the large Palace in the center of Berlin, where in peacetime the emperor had lived; the fight around *Vorwärts* was only part of the struggle that had broken out between the moderate wing of Social Democrats and the radicals. This struggle led to the split in the Social Democratic Party, and then early in January 1919 exploded in the revolt of the Spartacus League, a communist group led by Karl Liebknecht and Rosa Luxemburg.

During this revolt a good part of east and north Berlin were under Spartacist control. In the night the fire of machine guns could be clearly heard in our part of Berlin, the western side of the town. We knew what precautions had to be taken. Candles were distributed in every room because the electricity frequently failed. In the mornings, after we had washed, bathtubs were filled with water because it was feared that water might be cut off in the course of the day. Heat was limited to one room to save coal. The first few days, when we went out to get fresh air, we walked only a few steps up and down near our house. On these brief outings we usually met a family who had recently fled from Russia and was now living near us. The father had been a banker in Moscow but had frequently been in Germany, and the family was well known to my grandmother and my mother. I remember that when we heard the machine guns in the distance, they said: "Exactly as it was in Russia; that is how it begins." In fact, it did not begin. After a few days Spartacist control was reduced to a small part of Berlin; the shooting we heard became more and more distant. After the Christmas vacation ended I returned to school as if nothing had happened.

I know that I—and most of my acquaintances—were upset by the brutal and lawless manner in which the leaders of the Spartacist revolt, Liebknecht and Rosa Luxemburg, were killed by the government troops after they had been captured. But I was certainly pleased about the defeat of the revolt. I am inclined to think that the leading role of the Social Democrats in defeating the attack of the radical Left was a crucial factor in determining my adherence to the Social Democratic Party. Although in the coming months the extremists made attempts to come to power in the Rhineland, Bavaria, and the Ruhr, Berlin was no longer the center of the struggle. Moreover, concern soon shifted from domestic policy to foreign policy.

Like most of my contemporaries, and probably most Germans, I was indignant about the peace treaty that was presented to the German government early in May 1919. I regarded it as a violation of the assumptions under which the armistice had been concluded. I was against signing the peace treaty, although somewhat dishonestly, since I was relieved when the Reichstag produced a majority in favor of accepting the treaty.

Foreign policy remained the dominant political issue throughout the twenties. The question of reparations, which had not been settled in the peace treaty, became the center of bitter negotiations, most of all with France but also with the other Western powers. In the East, Soviet Russia presented an enigma. Its policy had two contrary faces: sometimes cooperation with Germany seemed its aim, sometimes extension of Communist rule over Germany.

Russia was then a focal point of German curiosity and interest. Frenchmen and Englishmen appeared in Berlin for special political or economic reasons, but social contacts between Frenchmen or Englishmen and Germans were out of the question in these postwar years. But Russian émigrés as well as representatives or agents of the Soviet government were well-known visitors in Berlin cafés. Recent Russian pamphlets, translated into German, could be found in book-stores or on the wagons of book vendors. I remember that in keeping with my interest in military affairs I bought brief treatises by Tukhachevsky and other Russian generals which set forth the principles of Marxist military strategy—such as the necessity of using tanks to reach the industrial quarters of cities quickly in order to combine military action with revolutionary upheavals of the working classes. There were other, not merely political reasons for the German curiosity about Soviet Russia. Russia was then a center for experiments in art and literature. This was the time of Lunacharski, the Soviet commissar for education, who favored modernism in every form.

When in June 1922 Mrs. von Simson, my mother's cousin, whose husband was then secretary of state at the German Foreign Office, telephoned saying that Chicherin, the Russian commissar for foreign affairs, would come to them for dinner and asked whether I wanted to come by after dinner and mingle for a while among the guests, I was enthusiastic. To see close up one of the leaders of the new Russia was highly exciting. I was astonished, however, when, after having been introduced to Chicherin, he invited me to sit down on the sofa next to him and asked me about my school. I embarked on a long defense of the humanistic Gymnasium— a topic more inappropriate for conversation with a leading man of the new Russian regime can hardly be imagined, and I still feel ashamed when I think about it. A few days later I heard from the Simsons that evidently Chicherin had engaged me in this long conversation because the negotiations he was conducting in Berlin had reached a point at which he preferred to avoid discussions with Walther Rathenau, then the German foreign minister, and officials of the German Foreign Office, who were also at the party. Although this explanation makes it clear why Chicherin wanted to spend time in an entirely insignificant conversation, this was not very flattering for me. I found Rathenau's presence at the party less exciting than Chicherin's because Rathenau was a part of the circle my family belonged to. My mother had known him quite well when he was a young man, and when I was introduced to him at the party he asked me to give her greetings and expressed his regrets at not having seen her recently. Because I expected to meet him at later occasions, all this seemed quite unimportant to me. This short encounter now stands clearly in my memory because, a few days later, Rathenau was assassinated.

The rise of anti-Semitism in Germany is frequently considered to be primarily responsible for Rathenau's assassination. In my opinion, this interpretation is shaped by what happened in Germany ten years later. At the time we did not consider anti-Semitism a decisive factor in this event. Certainly we were aware that those republican ministers who were Jews were attacked with unrestrained vehemence and hatred as corrupt, traitors, aliens, and I was familiar with some of the disgusting verses that gave expression to these feelings. It should not be forgotten, however, that non-Jews such as Mathias Erzberger, the leader of the Catholic Center Party, or Philipp Scheidemann, the leader of the Socialist Party who in November 1918 had proclaimed the republic from the balcony of the castle in Berlin, were also victims of the same political forces that assassinated Rathenau.

The wave of anti-Semitism was only one element in a much broader antirevolutionary wave that broke forth in the early twenties. Defeat and the armistice, the civil strife against

Communism, the peace treaty and the loss of territories, had all overshadowed and almost suppressed awareness of the internal changes going on in Germany. The groups and forces wedded to the old regime had never fully realized the shift in power that had taken place. They believed they could use every possible means to regain the power that, they thought, had slipped out of their hands not because the people had rejected their regime but under the pressure of external enemies. They were engaged in an antirevolutionary war. In my opinion Chancellor Wirth was entirely correct when, in a tribute to Rathenau after the assassination, he said, "The enemy is on the right." For my political education, for the intensification of my left-wing inclination, the assassination of Rathenau was of great importance. It revealed the stratum of amorality and lawlessness that formed a significant, almost permanent element of German rightist politics.

The Social Democrats, as I have indicated, had been a decisive factor in maintaining order and stability against extremism. But if the right refused to recognize that the revolution had taken place, those who accepted and approved the revolution—and I was certainly among them—felt that the revolutionary chapter was not yet closed. In many respects life went on as it had before the revolution. Class distinctions remained very noticeable, people continued to be carefully addressed with rank and titles, defeat had not extinguished the prestige of the military class, and there was a great display of wealth nourished by war profiteering and the onsetting inflation. Certainly the change of the regime had brought improvement in the situation of the working class: trade unions were legitimized and began to exert power and the grounds were laid for the development of a welfare state. However, Germany was not an egalitarian society and was still far removed from the realization of that perfect society at which the revolution had aimed.

Discontent, and a certain revolutionary ferment, remained

alive among the younger generation and found an outlet in literature, art, and the theater. We liked to read books and writers who had not yet been accepted into the official canon. I read Nietzsche at this time, and was more interested in his *Genealogy of Morals* because of its attack on bourgeois values than in his *Zarathustra*. Like many of my contemporaries, I read Freud, particularly his *Interpretation of Dreams* which seems to me worth mentioning because in England and the United States Freud's influence began to spread only much later. It was also at this time that I read Dostoievsky, in whom we thought we found something of Russia's revolutionary atmosphere; for me *The Idiot* was his most impressive work. However, reading it gave me the most terrifying dreams, and still does whenever I take it up again.

Under the empire modern art and literature had not been banned, but official disapproval was powerful enough to limit its impact to small groups of society. I remember the immense impression that the van Gogh exhibition of 1920 or 1921 made on me; it filled an entire building, the former Palace of the Crown Prince. The theater, likewise, was an exciting and revolutionary intellectual force in Berlin at the time.

The new Prussian government appointed a new head of the state theater, and thus, in one of Berlin's loveliest neoclassical buildings, the plays of Germany's classical authors were shown in startling revolutionary productions: Schiller's *Wilhelm Tell*, usually shown before a backdrop of snowy Swiss mountains and blue lakes, was performed on a bare staircase, so that its political message would come out clearly. There was much emphasis on works by contemporary authors who were writing expressionist dramas with titles like *Murderer of His Father* or *Not the Murderer, the Murdered Is Guilty*. These were either political, depicting the injustice of society, the misery of the downtrodden, and the desperation of the masses, or they were psychological, effacing the boundaries between the unconscious and the real. I suppose I am one of the few people still

alive who saw an early production of Bertolt Brecht's first
play, *Drums in the Night.* Brecht is the only playwright still
well known among those whom we found exciting at that
time. The others—Hasenclever, Bronnen, Toller—are almost
forgotten. The one I liked most is probably even less known
than the others: Fritz von Unruh. Son of a Prussian general,
educated in a cadet corps, an officer who had become an
opponent of war and violence, a friend of Walther Rathenau,
he expressed perhaps better than anyone else the atmosphere
of the time—its revolutionary hope and its entire lack of real-
ism. I still know by heart the words with which he concludes
one of his plays, and which proclaim his confidence in a "Kraft,
die aus neuer Liebe neue Menschen schafft" ("force which,
out of new love, creates new men").

INFLATION

I HAD passed the final examination of my humanistic Gymnasium (the *Abitur,* as it is called in German) in March 1923,
and in April I began to study in Heidelberg. A few days after
I had settled in my rented room, I went to the administrative
offices of the university to register and to sign up for the
lectures I wanted to attend. The offices were in a building on
Heidelberg's main street, and when I arrived a queue several
blocks long had already formed; it looked as if it would take
more than an hour before I could enter the building. I became
increasingly nervous when I noticed that several people had
been sent back and would have to line up the next day because
their papers were incomplete. Evidently a most careful examination of all the requisite papers—birth certificate, health
certificate, graduation certificate, etc.—was taking place. I
was not the tidiest person in the world and felt pretty sure
that I had forgotten documents I was expected to show, or
that my papers were not appropriately signed. Very timidly

I slipped my papers through the slit under the glass window. (I am still frightened when I have to deal with people who sit behind a counter and speak brusquely to the public through a small glass window.) The severe-looking university employee on the other side looked at my name, looked at me, and said: "Oh, the doctor's little boy from Baden-Baden" ("Das Büble des Herrn Hofrat aus Bode-Bode"). He immediately signed what he had to sign, and in hardly thirty seconds I was registered as a student at the University of Heidelberg.

By then my father had been dead for seventeen years, and it was nice to hear that he was still remembered. I was aware that he had been a well-known person in Baden. His family was English, but his father—my grandfather—who had been an officer in the English army, had settled in Germany after his retirement and married a German girl from the Rhineland. Thus my father had grown up in Germany and studied medicine at German universities. He settled in Baden-Baden where he became chief doctor and part owner of a sanatorium; he was frequently consulted by the grand duke of Baden, who spent his summers in the town. It had been the grand duke who had asked my father to become naturalized as a German because he did not want it to be said that he had "an English doctor." English doctors were not popular in Germany after the death of Emperor Frederick III in 1888: the emperor's death was widely attributed to a wrong treatment prescribed by an English doctor on whom the empress, the daughter of Queen Victoria, had relied.

The reminder that my roots were in Baden was a good beginning for my studies in Heidelberg. As much as I enjoyed being a member of the large Mendelssohn clan in Berlin, I placed a certain value on being recognized as a person in my own right; it gave me a feeling of independence, and I also enjoyed being able to claim that I was an heir to the liberal political tradition of Baden and not to Prussian authoritarianism. Thus whenever I am asked what part of Germany I come from I always say that I come from Baden, although truthfully the amount of time I have spent in that part of the world has been small.

What is foremost in my mind when I think of this first semester in Heidelberg is the extent to which I did things I liked to do. I remember mornings when I played tennis, or when, with my sketchbook, I climbed up the hill on which the old castle stands to draw the views. On hot days I played chess after the midday meal in a cool and dark restaurant, and drank one glass of the mild local wine after another. In the afternoons I walked to some quiet place along the Neckar where I could lie on my back in the water looking up at the trees lining the river bank and at the blue sky. In the evenings we bicycled to some inn on the plain between Heidelberg and the Rhine, with the hills that surrounded Heidelberg darkening, and the lights going on in the villages of the plain. "Der Abend wiegte schon die Erde und an den Bergen hing die Nacht." ("The eve was cradling earth to sleep and night upon the mountains hung"—Goethe.)

Actually my life in Heidelberg was not purely following my moods and whims. I gave a good part of my time to my studies. I took one seminar, paleography, which was given by Karl Hampe, a well-known medievalist, and I attended the lectures of some of the most famous Heidelberg professors, such as the philosopher Karl Jaspers, the literary historian Friedrich Gundolf, the sociologist Alfred Weber, and the art historian Carl Neumann. Alfred Weber's course on the "The Crisis of the Modern Idea of State" impressed me through its discussion of the dangers to which the democratic idea is exposed under the pressure of modern capitalism. This was six months after Mussolini's march on Rome. For the first time I became aware that Fascism was not, as I had thought, a strange, particularly Italian phenomenon but a danger inherent in industrialized society. The course that I enjoyed most and also remember best was Neumann's on "The

History of the German Town in the Middle Ages." The first four weeks of the course were concerned with Heidelberg as a model of the development of a medieval town. I learned why many streets were not straight but curved and why churches were built at particular locations. In 1923 the original medieval outline of the town was still clearly discernible; when I visit Heidelberg now it seems to have vanished.

It is easy to explain why I remember best those aspects of my life in Heidelberg I have just described, and why I enjoy recalling them. To remember that in life there are moments of pure delight and enjoyment was—and still is—a kind of defense against the harsh reality of life. The carefree and beautiful moments of my Heidelberg semester stand out with particular clarity and strength because they were in sharp contrast with the increasingly dark, grim atmosphere that enveloped Germany.

During my months in Heidelberg—from April to August 1923—inflation reached its height. The value of the mark declined from hour to hour. Every day after the closing of the stock exchange, when the new, always higher value of the dollar was announced, the shops raised the prices of their goods. In many respects I had it better than many others because, as I have recounted, I had received fifty dollars from my uncle before I left for Heidelberg. However, changing American dollars into German marks had its problems. Had I changed a large portion of the fifty dollars, the German money I received might have lost most of its value a few hours later. On the other hand it would have taken me a good part of each morning had I tried to change money daily, because people were always waiting in a long queue in front of the bank. Moreover if I exchanged currencies in the morning I might have lost a good part of what I received by the afternoon, when the new value of the dollar was announced. You did not need to be an economist to realize that you would do best if you bought goods as soon as you had changed your dollars into marks because the value of the goods you bought would rise along with the dollar and you could sell them when you needed marks.

I decided to buy pots of jam, an item that people liked and needed and that would never spoil. My rented room had a balcony looking out over the Neckar, and I filled this balcony with pots of jam that I sold from time to time. I was not the only student who tried to hold his own against inflation by immediately transforming marks into salable goods. This unending attempt to keep one's head above water created an atmosphere of restlessness, and the feeling grew that things could not go on much longer as they were, that some explosion or some breakdown would happen.

Pressure from external events increased the tension. My studies in Heidelberg began four months after the French had marched into the Ruhr district. The French had also occupied Mannheim, opposite Heidelberg on the other side of the Rhine, and their troops guarded the Rhine bridges. I am not sure whether visiting Mannheim required special permission and papers, but I recall going to Mannheim and staring, indignant and furious, at the French soldiers guarding the bridges. I also remember an evening when, with a few others, I was sitting, talking and drinking, in the room of a friend when suddenly another student appeared in great excitement: the French had fired on people bathing in the Rhine, and one Heidelberg student had been killed. Whether this was true I don't know, but we certainly believed that it could be true. I recall the story because it shows our insecurity and anxieties.

We were aware, of course, of the separatist movements in the north, in the Palatinate and the Rhineland. The lines dividing the German political parties from each other had become blurred. This was the time when the Communists, clearly in the hope of winning Germany as an ally against the capitalist countries, adopted a sharply patriotic tone. I attended

several political meetings at which the Communist representative sounded no less nationalistic than the advocates of the
extreme right. In contrast, Gustav Stresemann, who had always
appeared to be a man of the right, was one of the few voices
of moderation and reason. Almost every week he gave a speech
advocating a gradual abandonment of the struggle of the Ruhr,
and I still remember reading these speeches with astonishment because I had never expected him to be an advocate of
caution and compromise.

At the end of the semester, on my way back to Berlin, I
stopped in Nuremberg, where by chance the National Socialist Party was staging a great meeting just that day. For the
first time I saw numbers of flags with the swastika emblem
next to the black, white, and red flags of the Hohenzollern
Empire. At that time I did not think that National Socialism
could or would become a dominant influence in the Reich.
Its strong showing in Nuremberg seemed to me more a sign
that the catastrophic economic situation strengthened the
extremism of the Right and Left, and that the federalist
Bavarian government was happy to be the host of any movement that would weaken the Berlin government.

After the exhilarating and eventful months in Heidelberg,
being back in Berlin was a letdown; Berlin seemed colorless
and grim. It was entirely permeated by the mad, contradictory situation created by inflation. Wages and salaries were
continuously being raised, though less steeply than the decline
in value of the mark. People's earning were almost valueless,
but when they sold some of their possessions or shares they
received immense amounts of cash, and for a few days could
afford whatever they wanted. My mother was not allowed by
her brother, the banker, to sell anything; he advised her, very
wisely, that it was better to accumulate debts in marks than
to sell anything of real value.

Nevertheless, in this situation of mounting debt it seemed
difficult to justify her two grown-up children's doing nothing

but studying, and making no contribution to the household. I looked for a job. With the help of recommendations from friends I got a job in the Foreign Office as an assistant in the publication of Germany's prewar diplomatic documents. After the end of the war, the German republican government had "opened" the Foreign Office archives to refute the thesis that Germany alone bore the guilt for the outbreak of the war. The government had arranged to publish the most important documents from these archives. This developed into a much larger enterprise than had been originally planned. The work required almost ten years and led to the publication of fifty-four volumes. I worked in the Foreign Office for two years, from the fall of 1923 to the fall of 1925, when the stabilized economic situation made it possible for me to concentrate on my historical studies without having to earn additional money.

Admittedly I was very young, but this was not quite as exceptional as it might appear. I took the place of Hans von Dohnanyi, who twenty years later was executed because of his participation in the conspiracy against Hitler; Dohnanyi had also been a student when he went to work in the Foreign Office, but he left when his law examinations were approaching. Two other young historians were on the staff: one had just received his doctorate, and the other, Heinz Trützschler von Falkenstein, was still writing his dissertation. The archives employed young and inexperienced people because the budget assigned to the *Grosse Politik,* as this publication of the German Foreign Office archives was called, was so small. But we compensated for our youth and inexperience with our enthusiasm; we felt that we were engaged in an interesting and important undertaking. We were hardworking also because we labored under a very strict regime. The publication had three editors, but only one of them, Friedrich Thimme, was continuously present, selecting the documents, arranging their order, and writing explanatory footnotes. Thimme was trained as a historian, but because he was hard of hearing he had not been able to pursue a university career and had become a librarian. He was a typical Prussian civil servant: a strict disciplinarian, fair, and hardworking. With the regularity of a clock he appeared in the office at 8:30 A.M. so that he could be quite sure that we all would be at our desks at nine; he did not leave before 5:00 P.M., and so we couldn't either. Nevertheless, life in the office was less joyless than it might seem. We were all working in the same very large room; Trützschler and I soon became very good friends and because of Thimme's hearing difficulties we talked rather freely with each other and had our jokes.

Moreover, as I have mentioned, the work was exciting. At the beginning my activities were limited to inferior jobs like getting files from the lower floor where the documents were stored, reading proofs of the volumes that were being printed, and making indices. Later I began to write explanatory footnotes, and at the end I selected the documents and wrote the footnotes for a few chapters. The chapter on the early years of the German Baghdad Railroad was my work, and I am still quite proud of this early achievement.

It has been sometimes suggested that the *Grosse Politik* was biased in favor of Germany, that documents incriminating German policy had been left out. Such an intention did not exist; as a matter of fact, Trützschler and I—and the entire staff of the *Grosse Politik*—were very critical of the imperial policy and felt no reason to defend it. What has to be admitted is that the documents we used were chiefly those of the foreign policy section. We did not use documents of the economic section, which might have shown the influence of economic interests on the conduct of foreign affairs; this restriction undoubtedly contributed to a somewhat one-sided picture of German policy. Thimme himself would never have been willing to suppress documents, but, somewhat bored with years of editing, he was inclined to add to the documents long footnotes that went beyond comment and explanation into historical interpretation, presenting the German case. Often we had the amusing but also rather daunting diplomatic task of convincing him that one of his footnotes had to be toned down or shortened.

The two years in the Foreign Office archives were for me a busy, fruitful time. I met a number of younger historians in the archives who were studying in detail a particular episode in the history of the empire. One of them was Hajo Holborn, and this was the beginning of a friendship that continued in the United States, where, after 1933, Holborn became a professor at Yale, and ended only with Holborn's death in 1969. A further advantage of work in the Foreign Office archives was that it provided a unique training in historical techniques. I still find making an index an easy and quite satisfying job. There was a further intellectually useful aspect of my activity in the Foreign Office. I continued in the afternoons and evenings to attend a few lectures and seminars at the Berlin University. But since I felt rather sated with history, I chose topics like Italian literature, art history, and philosophy—topics somewhat outside my closest professional interests. Yet there was no doubt that my course was firmly set toward making history my profession.

Finally, in the fall and winter of 1923–24, there were personal advantages to having my days fully committed. Soon after I had begun work in the archives my mother died, and it was good not to have too much time for reflections about the world.

Strangely enough, in the same autumn of 1923 in which my own life took a new shape, the atmosphere in Germany changed. Revolts of the Left and the Right erupted—of Communists in Saxony and of the National Socialists in Bavaria—and were put down. Passive resistance in the Ruhr was abandoned, and a new currency was established after a radical devaluation of the mark. Thus, there came the opportunity to build a stable way of life, if on a much narrowed basis. Revolutionary dreams of creating a new world paled and vanished. Germany gained the aspect of a sound, middle-class country.

But for me—and I believe for many others whose crucial development occurred in the years between 1914 and 1923—a feeling of uncertainty about the world remained below the apparently firm surface. There was no stability in this world. Consequently, I have never been good in planning for the future, though in compensation I have had the advantage of being ready to face unexpected change.

Chapter III

Berlin in the 1920s

SINCE the end of the war, I have been in Berlin several times on brief visits. Cousins of mine and their children live there, and I have professional contacts with historians at the Free University. Whenever I am in Berlin now I am spoiled by friendliness and affectionate hospitality. Nevertheless, I feel insecure and disoriented, and somewhat uncomfortable. Although distress about the destruction and the changes that have taken place contribute to this feeling of discomfort, I am sure it is rooted in a less specific, more pervasive uneasiness. When I am in Berlin I am haunted by the impression that the ground on which I stand is not firm.

I ride a bus toward Zehlendorf, a western suburb. For a long stretch one side of the street is lined by a fence behind which are housed American troops protecting the status of Berlin. Then the bus enters an avenue that in the Berlin of my youth ran through a pine-wooded area, but that is now a busy thoroughfare between villas and large apartment houses. Suddenly I see a small house with one main floor built above a half-underground lower floor. The entrance door to which three steps lead up is in the center of the main floor, and on its two sides are three high windows formed by classical architraves that balance each other; clearly the house is a work of the early nineteenth century, of Berlin's neoclassical period. When I lived in Berlin I knew this house well; it had been a modest restaurant in which I and my friends frequently stopped on the way from Berlin to the lakes of Wannsee and Potsdam. It is still a restaurant, and the poster left of the entrance door indicating the beer they serve appears the same as it was fifty years ago.

The most altered, most unrecognizable part of present-day Berlin is the area around the Memorial Church and the Kurfürstendamm. Even in the first quarter of the century the generation of my grandmother regarded with some contempt the shops, the movie houses, the cafés and restaurants of this area as showy and lacking in elegance. But the shoddiness and cheap modernity of the newly constructed buildings, the noise and vulgarity of this tourist center, separate the present entirely from the past. I walk along the Kurfürstendamm with amusement, wonder, and disgust—that mixture of feelings the present world frequently arouses. I think that I now have reached the place where in former years I used to meet my friend Heinz Holldack—at the corner of the Kurfürstendamm and the side street in which he lived. The lower floor of the corner building now has glass shop windows and a flat, modernized facade, but then I look up and the upper part is still heavy Wilhelminian baroque, and there is still the corner balcony carried by some hefty, naked caryatides about which we hardly ever failed to make some disrespectful and, I fear, not particularly witty remarks.

I shy away from the Tiergarten area in which I once lived. The impenetrable rubble I found there in the spring of 1945 has been cleared, but not much construction has been done, and only a few buildings rise in isolation above the flat emptiness. There are still street signs, many of them carrying the same names as in the past, but nothing reminds me of the streets I knew, nor do they even seem to me to cover the same ground. In the middle of this stony plain there still stands the red and yellow sandstone Church of St. Matthew, not small, not large, compact and solid, exactly as the nineteenth century in which it was built imagined a church ought to look. Whether it was spared the destruction of bombs or restored, I don't know; to me it appears exactly as it was when, as a boy, I stood near its doors to look at the newly married couples and wave at acquaintances who were members of the wedding party.

These remnants of a former world—the beer house on the road to Potsdam, the caryatides on the Kurfürstendamm, the sandstone of the St. Matthew Church—are associated with no events of importance for me, but for this reason they affect me strongly. They appear to me to be alien elements in a world with which they have no connection. They make me terribly aware that quite a different world once existed and that I had been part of it. Whenever I am in Berlin, I become uncertain of where I am: in the city in which I once lived, or in the city in which I am now. Reality seems to slide out of my grasp.

Perhaps this is a useful experience for a writer of memoirs. In retrospect we are inclined to see in our lives links that connect past and present, to regard our reaction to sudden turns of events as the result of previous experiences, as shaped by the personality whose fundamental features were established in early years. I have grave doubts about this; I believe the situation into which you are placed, the events into which you are drawn and that overwhelm you, shape your life. What you yourself bring in plays only a very small role.

I

AFTER you have lived in a big city for some length of time
you are supposed to know it. Actually, it is only a small part
you know well; those streets you have walked, those houses
you have passed daily. It is only a small section of the entire
city that is *your city*.

The Berlin with which I was familiar was a limited area
within this big city of several million inhabitants. *My Berlin*
began at the old castle of the Hohenzollern, which stood at
the end of Berlin's parade avenue, Unter den Linden, and it
extended from there to the west, first through areas of apartment houses and shops, then through the suburbs of Grunewald, Dahlem, and Westend, up to the Havel River and the
Havel Lakes, where in Nikolassee, Wannsee, and finally
Potsdam the upper classes had their summer villas. My more
serious—let us call them professional—activities took place
in the area around Unter den Linden where the university
and the state (and university) libraries were situated, where
ministries and banks had their headquarters, and where most
of the theaters could be found. Friends and relations lived in
Charlottenburg, Grunewald, and Dahlem; these western parts
were the centers of my social life.

Between Unter den Linden and the residential areas of the
west, there was a middle section, the area around the church
built in memory of the emperor William I, which is still
standing as a ruin. Although my grandmother's generation
had their buying done in the old shops near Unter den Linden—Mosse and Grünfeld for linen and clothes, Borchardt
for food and wine, Friedländer for jewelry—my generation
frequented the modern shops in the streets around the Memorial Church, and I met my friends in this area when we went
out in the evenings. Here were the large and comfortable
movie houses, a few elegant restaurants, and many cafés which

in the summer placed their tables on the sidewalks behind
flower railings. Some of these cafés served ice cream soda,
regarded as a sensational new import from the United States.
There were many bars—a Russian bar, a French bar with
chairs placed closely together along the wall as in French restaurants, an Italian wine shop—and their popularity changed
from time to time.

In the early thirties my favorite bar, and the favorite bar
of my friends, was the Jockey: two or three relatively small
rooms on the ground floor of an apartment house near the
Memorial Church. The bar was in the back room; in the front
room was a piano; a young concert pianist who was a frequent
visitor of the bar would from time to time play classical music,
frequently Bach. The tables were close together so that you
could easily move and even talk from one to the other. One
of the acquaintances I made there was Erwin Planck, son of
the physicist. He had served as secretary of state in the Chan-
cellery under Papen and Schleicher, and was particularly close
to Schleicher. He left government service when Hitler replaced
Schleicher as chancellor, and was killed by the Nazis because
of his participation in the conspiracy against Hitler. At almost
any time of the day my friend Georg Federer, later a diplomat
in the Federal Republic, could be found sitting at the bar on
a high stool with a fat tome on his knees. He had decided
that the Jockey was the best place to study for his law examination.

From the Jockey it was a walk of hardly ten minutes to
where I lived, which was still the same apartment in which I
had lived as a schoolboy with my mother and grandmother.
My grandmother had continued to live there after the death
of my mother in 1923, and little had been changed in the
apartment. Several rooms—a large room in front and a dining room—were still furnished with my parents' furniture,
so that my sister and I considered the apartment as our own,
especially since for some short time we made a small contri-

bution to the payment of the rent. Occasionally, when I wanted
to work undisturbed, I rented a two-room apartment of my
own, but even then I took my meals at my grandmother's
and my bedroom there was always kept ready for me. The
bus passed in front of the house, and it was easy to take the
bus to the Memorial Church and the suburbs of the west or,
in the opposite direction, to the university. I could also walk
to the university through parts of Berlin's great central park,
the Tiergarten, and this took little more than half an hour.
Whether it is nostalgia or the memory of boyhood pleasures,
of all the big-city parks I have known, in Paris, in London,
and in New York, I have always considered the Tiergarten,
with its old trees, its wide avenues for horseback riding, its
many footpaths, and most of all its many large and small
lakes, the most beautiful.

In the 1920s I lived in the center of *my Berlin:* midway
between that section where the university and the theaters
were situated, and the section—farther out to the west—of
modern apartment houses and private villas. Now the wall
separating the West from Unter den Linden has cut *my Berlin*
into two parts—a further reason why, when I am in Berlin,
I feel on such uncertain ground.

II

MY Berlin was the bourgeois section of the city, and this was
the social world in which I moved. I knew a great many
people, but, as is generally the case, the basic substratum of
my social contacts was my family, more specifically my
mother's family, the Mendelssohns. Most of the descendents
of Moses Mendelssohn had continued to live in Berlin; they
were fundamentally a Berlin family. It was a very extended
family, but at the same time its members remained rather
close to each other. Conscious and proud of their Jewish heritage, but Christians since the beginning of the nineteenth

century, members of an upper social group, they had—to a
certain degree—kept apart and frequently intermarried.
Among the Mendelssohns people who considered themselves
cousins and felt close to each other would in other families
have hardly known of each other's existence. I should add
that at the end of the nineteenth and beginning of the twentieth centuries certain divisions had developed within the family
because some relations, nobilitated and very wealthy, had
tended toward high society, while others rejected this abandonment of a liberal tradition. However, after the First World
War, in the republic, these tensions disappeared.

Since the last years of the eighteenth century, when the
sons of Moses Mendelssohn had founded their banking house,
the family had spread into the most varied professions. There
were always bankers, but my grandfather had studied chemistry and had been a founder and first chairman of the AGFA
(Aktiengesellschaft für Anilinfabrikation), one of the great
German chemical companies. Since then, other members of
the family—two of my uncles, and later one of my Viennese
cousins—worked in the AGFA, or later in I.G. Farben when
the AGFA became part of this concern. But among my relations there were also civil servants, lawyers, and academics,
and some of the female members of the family had married
prominent doctors. Of course, these uncles and cousins made
many acquaintances and acquired new friends and connections in the course of their studies and professional activities,
so that family relationships brought me into a great variety
of social contacts.

One house where I met people from different spheres was
that of my grandmother's brother, Franz Oppenheim, who
was also my godfather. He was the chairman of the AGFA;
his wife was deeply interested in art, and I met scientists, art
historians, and painters in their house. A chief attraction of
dinners in that house was the collection of paintings Mrs.
Oppenheim had assembled. For a long time the family con-

sidered her crazy to have bought so many "awful" modern paintings. In the course of the 1920s, however, this contempt gradually turned to admiration for her courage in having followed her taste. The paintings are now dispersed, and I have seen some of them in American museums. Among them were *The White Roses* of van Gogh, *The Mail Coach* of Cézanne as well as a number of his watercolors, *A Lady Placing a Flower Vase on a Table* by Degas, and a *Lady in a Blue and White Dress with an Umbrella* by Manet. But among these paintings was also a *Madonna* by Greco and an unforgettable Guardi, *A Concert in the Doge's Palace.* It was a stunning collection, and its impressiveness was immensely enhanced by the manner in which the paintings were hung. In the winter they were in the Berlin house, but in the spring they were taken out to the summer villa in Wannsee. A dining room and various salons, all of them modest, some even small, looked out on the lake, and the paintings were distributed in these various rooms as ordinary wall decorations. You would talk after dinner, sitting in a living room around a small table on which there stood a lamp and a flower vase, and when you looked up your eyes fell on van Gogh's *White Roses.* When you went into the next room, perhaps to use a writing desk, you saw the Greco *Madonna* on the wall to the left of the writing desk. You did not see the paintings as showpieces; on the contrary, they caught you when you didn't expect it. They had a force of their own.

When I think of people whom I met through family connections, a costume ball in the house of my mother's youngest brother now stands out in my mind, because among the guests were people whom I met again many years later under entirely changed circumstances. Among them was a brother and sister couple, von Schultze-Gävernitz. I immediately fell in love with Miss Von Schultze-Gävernitz and asked her the next day whether she would be willing to marry me—an offer that in a very friendly but very decisive way she declined. I saw her again more than twenty years later when I was teaching at Bryn Mawr College and she was living with her husband in a suburb of Philadelphia. About the circumstances under which I met her brother again, when he was the assistant to Allen Dulles at the OSS, I shall report in a later chapter.

In the course of these years I met quite a number of people who played a role in German political or economic life, but meeting such people socially when you are a young student does not mean much. An evening I spent in the house of Max Alsberg might serve as an example. Alsberg was a well-known lawyer in Berlin who had a great reputation because of his role in some famous political trials. He was the defense lawyer in the trial initiated by Matthias Erzberger, a leader of the Catholic Center Party and finance minister of the republic, against the former vice-chancellor and Conservative leader Karl Helfferich, who had accused Erzberger of corruption. One day Alsberg telephoned, asking me to come to a party at his house. I was curious about this invitation and acccepted with alacrity. It emerged that the German jurists were meeting in Berlin, and Alsberg's party was for the leaders of the legal profession. Among them was the federal attorney general, Ludwig Ebermayer, who was supposed to be accompanied by his son, then at the beginning of a literary career. In order to entertain him Alsberg wanted to have some young people at his party. At the last moment, however, young Ebermayer did not appear. The luminaries of the legal profession—ministers of justice, professors, lawyers—were not interested in spending their time talking to a young history student. Consequently, I stood around, mute and uncomfortable.

Suddenly I saw a young man of my age who seemed equally lost. Eagerly we approached each other and then stopped: we were suddenly aware that we knew each other. Friedrich Meinecke, my history professor, lectured every morning at nine

in the university. At the first lecture of a semester you reserved
a seat for yourself by fixing your visiting card on the desk in
front of your seat. I had reserved for myself a very good seat
in the middle of the second row in order to hear well what
Meinecke was saying. But getting up early in the morning
was never to my liking, and I usually arrived only at the last
minute, sometimes even only as Meinecke was ascending the
podium. To get to my seat in the middle of the row all those
sitting closer to the aisle had to get up. I noticed that one
young man was getting up more and more slowly when I
passed by to take my seat. We had reached the point at which
I might have had to push him to get to my seat. This was
the young man at Alsberg's party, and we stared at each other.
Finally he or I said: "Tomorrow morning we shall have a
terrible fistfight." We laughed, began to talk, and withdrew
into a corner away from the company of the famous jurists.
This began my friendship with Arnold Haase, which has continued to the present day.

I do not want to give the impression that my life consisted
of going to dinner parties or attending formal family gatherings. The people among whom I moved and with whom I
was frequently, almost regularly, together were my contemporaries. They ranged in age from their early twenties to their
early thirties. Unlike the American and British systems where
college-age people spend three or four years together, usually
in a rather protected environment and isolated from the "real
world," German university students were regarded as grown
up and considered to be on equal footing with other people
at the beginning of their professional careers. Some of my
school or boyhood companions, including Theodor Mommsen,
Lothar Preuss, and Erich Wreschner, were then still in Berlin. In the historical seminar at the university I got to know
Heinz Holldack, and I continued to see frequently Heinz
Trützschler von Falkenstein, with whom I had worked in the
Foreign Office. (A later chapter will contain letters of all these

friends.) Then there were my two Vienna cousins, sons of my
mother's sister, who had married a Viennese doctor; one was
learning banking in Berlin, and the other was employed in
the AGFA. There were many other cousins, some younger
and some older, and, of course, all of them had their own
friends. Insofar as their professional activities were concerned
my friends were a mixed company: students, among whom
law students predominated; young lawyers; young civil servants, among them attachés in the Foreign Office; trainees in
banks and business enterprises.

On the other hand, I knew very few artists, and although
I was acquainted with quite a number of musicians whom I
encountered through my relations, they were usually older
and well established. There were exceptions: a young musician had been recommended to my grandmother, and he had
been invited for a Sunday midday meal. When, after the meal,
we had settled in the living room, he announced that he would
now like to give proof of his art, and he got up and began to
sing from great-grandfather's (Felix Mendelssohn Bartholdy's) *Elijah* the aria "Look down on us from heaven, O Lord."
Shortly after his recital, he left. About an hour later a young
man whom we did not know but about whom Swiss friends
had written us appeared for tea. We asked him what he was
doing in Berlin, and he said that he was studying singing,
and that he would be very glad to give proof of his art. We
were unable to dissuade him from this exercise, and so he
started: "Look down on us from heaven, O Lord." I believe
that we remained serious and civil until he left, but the door
had hardly closed when my sister and I broke down laughing.

Although the circle of contemporaries in which I lived was
divided by professional activities and interests, there was a
strong bond among us. We were—very definitely—a postwar generation. We felt we were different from those who
had grown up in the pseudo-splendor of the Wilhelminian
Empire and had taken part in the war. We actually disliked

stories about war experiences, although we were well aware that the soldiers had only done what duty demanded. But in our view the war had been a questionable business, and we considered it better to be silent about the role one had played in the war than to boast about it. We were pacifists, or at least pacifistically inclined, and happy that we were no longer living in a monarchy.

At the same time, however, formed in the turbulent years of defeat, revolution, civil war, and inflation, we had little belief in the duration of stability. The one certainty we had was that nothing was certain. Since none of the political movements that had started with the end of the war had fully reached its goal, we wondered whether unrest and turmoil was really abating or only reassembling for a new attack. On the other hand, we also differed from the generation that followed ours: those born in the second decade of the twentieth century. They grew up in the relative security of the second half of the twenties, and were much less conscious of the fragility of the social world than my generation. They were more demanding in what they considered their due, or Germany's due.

Nevertheless, the critical difference was whether one had grown up before 1914 or after. We felt strongly that the postwar generation was something new. We enjoyed shocking our elders by not wearing hats in the summer, by not wearing tuxedos when we went out in the evenings, and by sitting for long hours on high chairs in bars instead of going to suitable wine restaurants. We liked to live our own lives, not bound to firm, tight schedules. An incident comes to mind as rather characteristic of our behavior at this time. I used to work after supper and then go out around eleven o'clock to meet friends at a bar. On the way back I would eat a frankfurter at a street corner, or go to a café that was open twenty-four hours and served hot chicken soup. One icy winter night I entered this café, which was near the Memorial

Church, around 3:00 A.M. There, sitting in a heavy winter coat, was a friend of mine who, as I knew, lived in a rented room in an apartment above the café. I sat down with him and we talked—I suppose about people and politics—and, although I was still at the happy age when I needed little sleep, I decided at around four that it was time to go home. My friend said to me: "I can't go up to my room; I have to sit here till the morning." While saying this he opened his heavy coat and I saw that underneath it he wore nothing but his pyjamas. He explained that he had been together with a girl in his room, and when he had accompanied her downstairs and said good-bye to her in front of the house, the door had slammed shut behind him. As was customary in Berlin at that time, the doorman left around ten in the evening and returned only the next day at eight in the morning. After ten at night you could enter the house only with your own key, and my friend had not taken his key along to the farewell at the house door. He was a lucky man to have on the ground floor of his house a café that was open twenty-four hours, where he could sit until the doorman appeared in the morning to resume his functions.

Of course, there were other ways of getting together late in the evening. My eldest uncle had given me a car, a little Opel, which had previously belonged to his daugther, who was called Baby in the family. When the car had been new, my uncle had had the hood plate with Opel on it replaced by one with Baby on it. When I got the car the plate remained, thus distinguishing it from dozens of other little Opels in Berlin. In the late afternoon and on the long summer evenings I could drive out to the lakes, but the car had also another use: friends, seeing "Baby" parked on the street while I was in a restaurant or movie, could leave notes on the windshield letting me know where they would be so that, later on, I could join them.

I have often wondered whether, as it is frequently said, the

First World War brought about a great change in sex morals. Certainly we all had read our Freud; although such reading sharpened our psychological understanding, I don't think we believed that our lives and actions were dominated by sex. Actually, if I reconstruct my own attitude and those of my contemporaries correctly, we had a rather simple attitude with regard to questions of sex and sexual morality, which was to let everyone do what he or she wanted to do, and to talk as little as possible about the sex morals of other people. This had its particular bearing upon homosexuality. Berlin had the reputation of leaving homosexuals undisturbed, and accordingly, the city was popular among homosexuals. Foreigners visiting the city usually wished to see something of the amorality of Berlin life about which they had heard so much. Consequently, Berliners—and I was no exception— often guided visitors to a restaurant and large dance hall frequented exclusively by homosexuals. The foreigners usually went away happily content that they now could talk on the basis of personal experience about the licentiousness of the city. Actually, homosexuality played a small role in Germany; on the basis of later observations, I would say a much smaller role than in England. In Prussia homosexuality had been proscribed by the criminal code since the early nineteenth century, but it was official policy not to apply the relevant paragraph. We, of course, knew people or couples who were homosexuals, but it was not a topic of discussion or particular interest, and as far as I can judge, it did no harm to the social positions or the professional careers of these people.

What seemed to me predominant in our attitude to questions of sex and morality was the demand for a certain honesty. We despised the nineteenth-century attitude that treated women of different classes differently, suggesting that one should go to bed with a woman of one class, but marry a woman of another. The essential requirement in the relation between sexes seemed to us the presence of a true affection. If that was there it seemed to us no great difference whether a couple lived together for a while and then either got married or separated, or whether, if they were more conventional, they began to live together only after they had gotten married.

In our consciously held views and attitude we were probably quite "modern," but it must also be said that the outward forms of social life, at least among the bourgeoisie, were still quite conventional: marriages were celebrated with all the traditional solemnity, and divorces, although becoming more and more frequent, were still considered to be a minor catastrophe. My grandmother was deeply unhappy when one of her granddaughters got a divorce, although later on she became more resigned to it. A student friend of mine who lived together with a female student frequently visited our house, and the couple was very popular with my grandmother; but I never would have dared to tell her that they lived together.

The attitude of my grandmother was not so much an expression of a particularly Victorian outlook, but more the reflection of "official," generally accepted attitudes. Moreover, in some way this parting of actual behavior and publicly accepted values may be considered characteristic of contrasting attitudes that had developed in Germany in the twenties. Revolution and inflation in Germany, which had encouraged radical convictions and notions more quickly and strongly than in other countries, also strengthened a belief in the need to maintain traditional customs and values.

III

IN THE years about which I am writing, the 1920s, my main interests were historical scholarship and politics.

After the end of my work as an assistant to the editors of

the German Foreign Office documents, I studied for a year in Munich. By then the political turmoil that had exploded in the Hitler putsch of 1923 had subsided, and Munich had sunk into a quiet provincialism. I remember some posters announcing that Adolf Hitler, now out of prison, would speak at a public meeting, but it did not enter my mind to go because at the time Hitler and his movement seemed to be utterly unimportant. Still, despite the lack of excitement, living in Munich—a lovely city set in a beautiful landscape— was highly enjoyable, and the year there was also intellectually profitable. In a seminar given by a law professor, Karl Rothenbücher, who had been a friend of Max Weber, we read Weber's *Wirtschaft und Gesellschaft (Economy and Society)* from beginning to end, and in another seminar given by a young philosopher we studied very precisely Hegel's *Phänomenologie.* Yet, although Munich had its attractions, I had no doubt that I wanted to complete my historical studies in Berlin. The reason was the presence of Friedrich Meinecke at Berlin University. Meinecke had shaken up German historical scholarship by emphasizing the relations among intellectual movements, political thought, and political action; after working for two years in diplomatic documents I was eager to broaden my outlook on the past. In addition, among the many conservative and reactionary German professors, Meinecke was an exception: he was a defender of the republic. Moreover, while I was working in the Foreign Office I had come to know several students of Meinecke, and I had heard from them that he allowed his students a very free hand, though at the same time was very much interested in what they were doing.

Meinecke was a great teacher. Although he stammered, and his lectures were rhetorically undistinguished, they were beautifully organized, and in placing the events of national histories in a European context they continued a tradition of German historiography that had begun with Leopold von

Ranke. Meinecke's seminars provided a rigorous training in historical methodology. They focused on the art of interpretation. We usually discussed a single document or treatise, like the French Charter of 1814, or Machiavelli's *Prince,* and subjected the meaning of each sentence, almost each word, to scrutiny and discussion. Half of each seminar was taken up with the reading of papers written by the participants on the document under investigation. After a paper was presented Meinecke usually did not say more than "Thank you," but when he added "Good," you believed you were in seventh heaven.

Some members of the seminar were most reluctant to open their mouths because they did not want to confront Meinecke with what might be an inappropriate contribution to the discussion. Although, in my opinion, this was a silly attitude, it shows something of Meinecke's immense prestige and authority among history students. Those who attended his seminar knew that in the evaluation of a historical work quality was his only concern; he was entirely impartial, and his judgments were uninfluenced by ideological considerations. Meinecke's attitude toward the work of Eckart Kehr is a good example of this. Kehr, after the Second World War, attained posthumous fame as a pioneer in the application of methods of social history and social criticism to German history. In the late twenties, when I was studying in Berlin, Kehr had just finished his dissertation on the building of the German navy; in contrast to the traditional doctrine about the primacy of foreign policy, it set forth the thesis that the navy owed its existence to a compromise between the interests of the great landowners and the leaders of heavy industry. Meinecke was not particularly enthusiastic about this demonstration of the determining nature of material interests in the foreign policy of the empire. But he was so impressed by the quality of Kehr's research that he did something very unusual: in the book he was then writing on the origins of the conflict between Germany and Great Britain, he praised Kehr's manuscript, which was still unpublished.

I knew Kehr quite well. He was a most astonishing mixture of high intelligence and naïveté. He came from a family of Prussian civil servants, and had inherited something of their ascetic attitude. He was full of distrust of wealth, and was inclined to believe that wealthy people must be evil. On the other hand, he believed that when confronted with the truth, people would accept it no matter what their prejudices, traditions, and interests might be. He saw himself as starting a new, modern movement in German historiography, and there is no doubt that he appeared to many of us as the born leader of a new generation of historians.

Because of Meinecke's presence, the historical seminar of the University of Berlin was the center of gravity for history students with a democratic and intellectually adventurous outlook. This attitude was not popular among older, conservative historians, still predominant in German academic life. On the occasion of Meinecke's retirement (I believe it was in 1931), a meeting in his honor was arranged in the Berlin seminar, at which his older and younger disciples were present. Kehr and I had written a play in which we made fun of the various patriotic myths of German history (I must confess that Kehr wrote the more satirical and amusing parts, whereas I moderated the tone by inserting here and there patriotic and sentimental verses). I have no doubt that this play was a sorry effort, but the openly expressed contempt of Meinecke's older disciples, whose admiration for the master had been expressed in a very traditional eulogy, was aroused not so much by the lack of quality of our dilettantish poetry as by its lack of respect for the heroic stories of the past and by our radicalism.

In this atmosphere of pervasive academic conservatism, "habilitation" (acquisition of the right to lecture at a university as *Privatdozent,* i.e., without salary—the first step in the

academic hierarchy) was at many universities not easy to attain for a young scholar of left-wing views. For this reason,
although it was unusual to have several *Privatdozenten* working in the same discipline at the same university, Meinecke
"habilitated" several of his students in Berlin. When I
passed my doctor's examination in 1931, one of the Berlin
history professors, Fritz Hartung—an excellent scholar and
teacher, so strictly conservative that he was obedient to
whoever was ruling—said: "I probaby shall have to give you
a gold watch." And when I looked at him with puzzle-
ment, he added: "I have promised to give a gold watch
to the twentieth Meinecke student to be habilitated in
Berlin."

I have often been regarded as a characteristic product of
the Meinecke school, and am thought to have been close to
him. This is not so. Although a good part of my work has
been concerned with what is called the history of ideas, I have
also worked in political, social, and military history. Moreover, in the early years of my scholarly activity I was personally not very close to Meinecke. Of Meinecke's students who,
after 1933, emigrated and settled in the United States, Hajo
Holborn, Dietrich Gerhard, and Hans Rothfels were certainly much closer to him than I ever was.

Meinecke did show some special interest in my dissertation, which dealt with the political and historiographical ideas
of Johann Gustav Droysen, one of the great, many-sided
nineteenth-century German historians. Droysen had worked
in classical history (he was the creator of the term "Hellen-
ism"), in philosophy of history, and in modern political history; he had been a professor in Berlin, and Meinecke had
heard his lectures. This subject had not been my first choice.
When the time came for me to see Meinecke and discuss with
him a subject for my dissertation, I proposed as a topic "The
Origin of the Idea of Balance of Power in the Renaissance." I
had made two or three short trips to Italy, and the Renais-

sance had become my great love. Moreover, I was attracted by this subject because—partly as a result of my work in the Foreign Office—I was intrigued by the working of international relations, in which the idea of balance of power is a key concept. In response to my proposal Meinecke looked at me rather quizzically and said: "You know, Mr. Gilbert, the handwritings of that period are very difficult; none is exactly like the other. They are very individual. Wouldn't it be better if you would take a topic closer to our time, perhaps a topic of nineteenth-century history, and work in Renaissance history after you have done your dissertation?"

Thus, more or less accidentally, Meinecke set the course I have followed throughout my life: to work in nineteenth-century intellectual history as well as in Renaissance history. But I did not foresee that at the time. On the contrary, I left Meinecke's house somewhat discouraged. A few days later I met my friend Hajo Holborn and told him the story. He said that he had seen Meinecke not long before and that Meinecke had spoken with great interest of a recent publication of papers by Droysen on the revolution of 1848. Holborn suggested that I might propose Droysen as the subject for my dissertation. It proved to be a particularly fortunate choice because two years later Droysen's correspondence was published; the correspondence fascinated Meinecke and he reviewed it in a lengthy essay. Meinecke, therefore, was particularly interested in my dissertation, and I had probably more than the usual number of discussions with him about it. In one of these interviews, during which I had stressed the influence of Hegel on Droysen, which Meinecke denied, I said: "But Hegel was a great historian," and Meinecke pounded his fist on the desk and said: 'No, that he was not!''

There was another episode that established a somewhat closer connection between Meinecke and me. After having finished the dissertation it was customary in Germany for the doctoral candidate to go to the professors who would examine him

and arrange a date for the oral examination. The establishment of an examination schedule usually took place four to
six weeks before the examination. I went to Meinecke early
in January, soon after the Christmas vacation, and after I had
explained to him the purpose of my visit I asked him when
in February or March he would have time to examine me.
Meinecke said: "I am free now. How is it if I would examine
you now?" For a moment I was shaken, but then I thought
that it would be ridiculous to tell the professor with whom I
had studied modern European history for four years that I
would be ready to be examined in this field only after I had
studied it for another four weeks. I therefore said that if he
had time to examine me now, this would be fine with me.
Once the examination was over I concluded that it hadn't
gone too badly because, after the hour of questions, Meinecke
said: "Do you really think it would have been much better
four weeks later?" And I left Meinecke's house somewhat elated
because, whereas I had expected in the following four weeks
to devote my time to modern European history, I could now
spend all my time preparing for examinations in my minor
fields: medieval history, philosophy, and economics.

The next morning my friend Mommsen telephoned. He
told me that the evening before, his mother had been at a
party with Mrs. Meinecke, who had mentioned that her husband had been most pleasantly surprised that afternoon. After
asking doctoral candidates from time to time over the last
thirty years whether they would be willing to be examined
immediately rather than arranging a future date, he had for
the first time found a candidate who had agreed to this proposal. Later Meinecke alluded several times to this event. If
it contributed to establishing a closer connection with him,
this connection was not based on my scholarly qualities but
on my intellectual impudence.

In any case, the end of my studies for a doctorate in history
was satisfactory. A few weeks after the examination Meinecke

offered me the job of editing the political writings of Droysen for the Prussian Academy. He also indicated that he thought I might pursue a university career, and that it was not necessary for me to take the state examination, which would have entitled me to teach at a Gymnasium. At that time I was highly pleased, but from a practical, financial point of view it turned out to be bad advice. If I had sat for the state examinations I would have, after 1945, received a pension as if I had been an active civil servant throughout the entire Nazi period.

Meinecke never became a Nazi, nor did he lose contact with friends and students who had to leave Germany. But in the thirties he never gave much expression to his disapproval of the Nazi regime; he tried hard to find positive features in it and he looked upon the Nazis as a powerful, dynamic force. This attitude did not surprise me, nor do I think it surprised many of his other students. Meinecke called himself "a republican by reason." The republic seemed to him the appropriate form of government after the First World War, but his heart was not in the republic. He once asked me as elections approached whether I would be willing to do some work for the Democratic party. He was somewhat shocked when I said that I was willing to help but that I did not vote the Democratic Party, I voted Socialist. It must also be said that although no Jew had difficulties in being accepted among those who wrote dissertations under him, I think he supported habilitation only of those Jews who had converted to Christianity. Meinecke came from a traditional, conservative background, and it was not surprising that traces of this background remained. It is astonishing how far he had gotten in overcoming this background and opening himself to other ideas: liberalism, democracy, and nonconfessional religiosity. And it should also not be overlooked that what was a weakness in his political outlook was tied to what was characteristic and, one might say, a strength in his historical approach:

its relativism, its emphasis on judging a past time on the basis of its own values, a subtle recognition of the continuous change in values. Such an attitude does not lead to very strong convictions and beliefs in politics. It must be admitted that, although historians are fatally attracted to politics, historians are not necessarily good politicians.

I saw Meinecke again briefly after the war. During the summer of 1945, while stationed at the headquarters of the Office of Strategic Services in Wiesbaden, I passed through Göttingen on my way to a meeting in Hannover. I had heard that Meinecke had been evacuated from Berlin to Göttingen, and after a lengthy search I got his address at the office of the municipal police. It was after 2:00 P.M. when I reached the apartment house where the Meineckes were staying. After I had rung the bell I told the maid who answered that I would like to see Professor Meinecke, but the maid told me that this was impossible; this was the time of the professor's siesta, and he could not be disturbed. I said with some emphasis that she should ask the professor whether he could not spare time for me, and gave her my name. She went to the next room, leaving the door somewhat open. I heard her saying to Meinecke, "There is an American officer who wants to see you. His name is Gilbert." I heard Meinecke say: "No, no, Gilbert, Gilbert, I don't know anyone with that name. I know only one Gilbert and he is in America." I shouted, "No, he is in Göttingen," and then I was admitted. The visit was very short because I had to be in Hannover in the evening. We talked about Meinecke's experiences during the war, and about what had happened to people with whom I had studied history in Berlin in the twenties and early thirties. I was pleased that Meinecke remembered my interest in the Renaissance and wanted to know how my studies in this field had progressed.

IV

NOBODY who lived in Germany in the twenties and early thirties could escape politics. When I say that in these years politics was an absorbing interest of mine I do not claim that this distinguishes me from my contemporaries.

I have mentioned that the overthrow of the empire in 1918 had created an unstable situation: those who had formerly ruled were unwilling to accept the change and opposed, in legal and illegal ways, the new rulers. Tension continued and was heightened by struggles over the many problems the end of the war and the Peace of Versailles had created: reparations, the occupation of the Rhineland, the disarmament of Germany.

Though in turmoil throughout the 1920s, German politics varied in the extent of its instability. In the second half of the decade, the road seemed to be relatively smooth; from 1929 on, however, it went steadily downward. There were many reasons why the year 1929 represented a turning point. One event has always seemed to me of particular importance: in 1929 Gustav Stresemann died. Originally I was very distrustful of Stresemann because of his nationalistic attitude during the First World War, when he had been a proponent of German expansionism. I distrusted him also because the party he led, the German People's Party, was the main advocate of heavy industry. Stresemann seemed to me the embodiment of autocratic special interests concerned with the pursuit of their own economic advantages. Gradually, however, I began to recognize that either my view of him was oversimplified, or he had undergone a kind of conversion after his superpatriotic days of the First World War. As a student in Heidelberg in the spring of 1923 I could not but admire the courage of speeches in which he advocated the end of the economic resistance to the French in the Ruhr. While studying in Munich in 1926 I attended a large public meeting in

which Stresemann defended his foreign policy, and I noticed
with approval something entirely unexpected: even the Germans could produce a great public orator.

I came to a full appreciation of his personality, however,
only after a direct encounter. In the historical seminar of Berlin University I had come in closer contact with Theodor
Eschenburg, who was then also a history student. Eschenburg had founded a kind of political club called the Quirites,
in which, with the exception of right-wing radicals and Communists, all political parties were represented. One of its purposes was to counteract the deepening tension among the
political parties, which made political compromise—and in
the German multiparty system, that meant government in
general—impossible. Twenty to thirty relatively young people—among them ministry officials, attachés in the Foreign
Office, lecturers from the university or the School of Politics,
a few people from banks, business, and trade unions, and
students—assembled monthly to have dinner together. Usually a guest, either an active politician or a person of political
influence, was invited. Eschenburg, who was closely acquainted
with Stresemann, arranged to have him as the guest at one of
our meetings. By then Stresemann had been foreign minister
for four or five years.

The frankness with which Stresemann discussed the political situation and the interest with which he listened to our
opinions was surprising. He showed none of the condescend-
ing attitude of a high German official who gives you to
understand that he knows things better, and that you still
have a lot to learn and should listen carefully to him. What
Stresemann said about foreign policy entirely lacked the
nationalistic note that could sometimes be found in his public speeches, in which he might have found a nationalistic
appeal necessary for propagandistic reasons. On this evening
he showed a remarkable appreciation of the difficulties the
French had in making concessions to Germany. The most

interesting moment came when Stresemann was asked how
he felt about a suggestion frequently made at that time: to
make a constitutional change that would give more power to
the president of the republic. Stresemann's rejection of this
suggestion was emphatic: "What, more power to the president? What nonsense. He has already much too much power."
I got the impression that Stresemann was truly a parliamen-
tarian; he really wanted the parliament to rule. At that time
I found it most encouraging that one of Weimar's most powerful politicians fiercely believed in the necessity of maintaining a parliamentary system in Germany. In retrospect I am
convinced that his death represented a fatal blow to democracy in Germany. It removed from the bourgeois camp the
most powerful voice in favor of the parliamentary system.

After Stresemann's death in 1929, the cabinet in which he
had been foreign minister continued for a few months, and
then Heinrich Brüning became chancellor. Brüning had no
clear parliamentary basis and ruled with emergency decrees;
the formation of the Brüning government marked a crucial
step away from democracy toward authoritarianism. This is
not hindsight but was clear to everyone who looked upon the
political scene without illusions. The opposon to Brüning's
"rule by emergency decrees" proceeded very cautiously and
avoided actions that might have resulted in an open break
between the government and the Reichstag. The maintenance of a semblance of legitimacy, it was thought, might
make possible a return to full parliamentarism in the future.
Thus one "presidential government" ruling by emergency
decree followed the other; after Brüning came Papen, after
Papen, Schleicher, and after Schleicher, Hitler. I have never
understood why Brüning, who had initiated this vicious circle, was later received in the United States as a wise states-
man who could give advice about the policy to be pursued
toward Nazi Germany.

A change in Germany's political atmosphere was soon

noticeable after Brüning came to power. There was a resurgence of nationalism and a sharpening of the tension between Right and Left, between the bourgeois camp and the parties representing the trade unions and the workers. This change in the political climate became evident to me at a meeting of the Quirites. In 1931, in order to demonstrate that it had infused new energy into German politics, the Brüning government had agreed with Austria on a German-Austrian customs union. A few days later a meeting of the Quirites took place at which this event formed the main issue of discussion. I said what seemed to me obvious: that this action was a serious mistake because the French could not allow formation of a customs union, which would be regarded as the first step toward the *Anschluss;* the action would end in a defeat of Germany, an entirely unnecessary demonstration of Germany's helplessness. I was entirely unprepared for the storm aroused by my words, which seemed to me pure common sense. It was indicated that my view reflected a despicable, un-German attitude. I was quite upset. In this group which for several years had quietly discussed political issues suddenly a line was drawn separating certain views and attitudes as German from others that were condemned as non-German. I had a presentiment that this was a taste of things to come.

The next stage on the way downward was the formation of the Papen government in 1932. My views of Papen had been formed by a chance encounter with him one afternoon in the late twenties. I was visiting relations of mine in Dahlem. The husband was absent but was expected home soon. He finally appeared along with a tall, elegant gentleman whom he had met at the races and whose name—von Papen—did not signify much at that time. Papen had come along because he and the relations whom I was visiting were all going to the same dinner party in the neighborhood. While my relations were in the house getting ready for the party I was left alone with Papen in the garden, and we talked for about half an

hour. No weighty subjects were discussed. We talked about
Paris, which I had visited a few weeks before, and Papen
quickly agreed with me that Paris was a very beautiful city.
So it went on, with Papen happily agreeing with every banal-
ity that came into my mind. I have no clear recollection of
what else we talked about, but this does not mean that I
didn't get a definite impression of Papen. A few years later I
saw at a newspaper kiosk that Papen had been appointed
chancellor, and I said to my friend Holldack, who was standing next to me: "That is impossible; he is a complete light-
weight." This shows how wrong a slapdish judgment can be,
or perhaps how right it can be.

The fatal "achievement" of the Papen regime was the dep-
osition of the Prussian Social Democratic government in July
1932. This action removed the last serious obstacle to the
establishment of an authoritarian right-wing regime. When
the removal of the Prussian government was announced I went
with friends to one of the Prussian ministries, where we knew
some of the higher officials. We expected them to be in contact with trade union leaders and to proclaim a general strike;
we wanted to find out whether we could be of help. A general
strike had been successful ten years before in defeating the
rightist Kapp putsch and seemed the last hope in the present
situation. Of course we were not the only people who tried
to persuade the deposed members of the Prussian government
to initiate this kind of action, and we received the same answers
as others making similar recommendations: "How can you
proclaim a general strike in a time of economic crisis and
rising unemployment? The jobs of the strikers will be immediately filled by the unemployed." I was not then—and I am
not now—convinced of the soundness of this argument. A
general strike might have been more effective than was believed
at the time. It was moreover a necessary gesture, a warning
that democracy would not go down without a struggle.
Nevertheless, since the Left had abandoned one position after

the other during the three preceding years, it was perhaps difficult to recognize the crucial importance of this particular action—that the removal of Prussia's Socialist government meant the loss of the last position of power from which the Socialists could influence the course of events.

So far in these reminiscences of the political developments of the twenties, I have only mentioned the most outstanding events and my reactions to them. I have hardly touched upon what was really a determining factor: the atmosphere in which these events took place. The second half of the 1920s were years of economic upswing and prosperity, and then, after 1929, followed the economic crisis and decline, steadily accelerating and gradually enveloping the entire nation in gloom. The impact of the economic crisis on me personally was limited. I realized that the prices of my shares were steadily declining, but since I could not live on their income anyway, the practical consequence was only that I was forced to sell more of them if I wanted to go on living as I had before. Of course, I was aware that the prospects of life had narrowed, that everyone struggled not for goals to be reached in the future but to get through the next day. I noticed the disappearance of small shops at which I had been a customer since my childhood. Young people about whom I knew because their parents had been minor employees in small firms with which I had had some dealing were abandoning the idea of studying and were happy to get occasional menial jobs. Acquaintances cut down their expenses more and more in order to support relations who had gotten into difficulties. We were kept aware of the continuously darkening economic horizon by the weekly publication of the steadily rising unemployment figures. I shall always remember the feelings of anxiety with which I opened the newspapers on the day when these statistics appeared.

The crisis and the accompanying shift in political power had consequences that were of very personal concern for me:

the confidence and aggressiveness with which conservative and reactionary forces came to dominate the academic scene. The Prussian Ministry of Culture and Education, which supervised the universities, had been directed since 1918 by a man of a courageously liberal outlook, and the fall of the Prussian government had a deep impact, therefore, on the academic prospects of individuals. An example of the difficulties that now developed for scholars on the political Left was the case of Eckart Kehr. When I first got to know him he had had no doubt about his academic prospects and saw himself, as I have mentioned, as the leader of a new historical school. He was still full of fight when the Brüning government came to power. He, my friend Holldack, and I spent many evenings discussing the founding of a historical-political journal. The choice of the title, *Historisch-Politische Zeitschrift* (Historical-Political Journal), was a slightly ironic and also provocative reminder of the historical-political journal that Ranke had edited one hundred years before. We intended to emphasize that political action, whether in foreign or domestic policy, was the result not of a pure *raison d'état* but of the struggles of interests—economic, social, and ideological; we wanted thereby to counter the nationalistic and romantic myths about the past that began to be more and more propagated and accepted. After we had arrived at some outline of how we wanted this periodical to look and had talked to a publisher, the project proved to be unfeasible for financial reasons.

Then, in 1931–32, I spent some time in Italy. When, back in Berlin, I met Kehr, he was a changed person: less ebullient, somewhat bitter. His dissertation—and then a number of brilliant, provocative articles in the socialist periodical *Die Gesellschaft*—had been sharply criticized by traditional historians. He was now working on Prussian policy in the Napoleonic era, and he believed he had noticed that the archivists were not being particularly accommodating and helpful. He had come to realize that he might encounter dif-

ficulties in the pursuit of an academic career, and he had
decided to go to the United States for a year. He was apply-
ing for a Rockefeller Fellowship but felt uncertain about the
outcome. I soon heard more about this application. My uncle,
Albrecht Mendelssohn Bartholdy, professor of international
law at Hamburg and director of an Institute for Foreign Policy there, was a member of the Rockefeller committee.
Whenever he was in Berlin he usually came to have a meal at
my grandmother's. Soon after I had talked to Kehr I saw my
Uncle Albrecht at my grandmother's and he asked me to
accompany him since he wanted to discuss something pri-
vately with me. He told me that he was in Berlin for a meeting of the Rockefeller committee, and a vehement discussion
about the application of a historian, Eckart Kehr, was taking
place. "Good old Meinecke," as my uncle said, had written
a very favorable recommendation. But there were letters in
which Kehr was called irresponsible, radical, and biased. I
assured my uncle of Kehr's great talents and thereby confirmed him in what he wanted to do: take up the fight for
Kehr. Kehr got the fellowship, but he was by then already a
sick man and died in the United States.

One could no longer fail to notice that for people who were
antagonistic to the rise of nationalism and authoritarianism—even for those lacking Kehr's missionary spirit—the
pursuit of an academic career was becoming very difficult.
One could not overlook the fact that there were many aspiring historians who were better fitted to the spirit of the times.
During these years I was particularly close to my friend
Holldack, and although we did not give up the plan to pursue an academic career, we thought that it might be wise to
prepare a fall-back position. Journalistic work appealed to us
as an interesting and even exciting temporary occupation.
Holldack went on to become a full-time journalist. I had
some contacts with the *Frankfurter Zeitung* and published in
it a few short reports about Italian cultural events and about

the Fascist financial policy. But these contacts ended in 1933.

I don't want to give much weight to these journalistic plans. They were signs of the anxiety with which we looked upon the course of events in Germany. But in all honesty I must say that neither I nor Holldack was really ever convinced that we would have to give up our plans for an academic career. This we realized only after the curtain had fallen.

V

IT HAS frequently been forgotten that for several years after the First World War Germans had little contact with the outside world, for both political and economic reasons. This changed in the middle of the twenties when the reparations question was settled and the Locarno treaties had been concluded. Then the gates to the outside world stood open again. Paris especially became the goal of German pilgrimages. Writers as different as Fritz von Unruh and Thomas Mann wrote enthusiastically about what they had heard and seen on their first visits to Paris after the war. I was in Paris for the first time in the fall of 1926; I was attending the wedding of one of my Viennese cousins, who married the daughter of the Austrian ambassador to France. I was as overwhelmed by Paris as anyone else. I arrived by train very early in the morning and took a cab to my hotel. On the way we crossed the Champs Elysées. At this time of day the avenue was still quite empty; to the left the view reached the Louvre, and to the right the Arc de triomphe. In the clear light of the morning sun, under a light-blue sky, this seemed the most grandiose view I had ever seen and would ever see. I stayed in Paris only a few days, but I found them utterly exciting. In my enthusiasm for French literature I then subscribed to the *Nouvelle Revue Française,* and for some time, with appropriate vanity, I pretended to be an expert in modern French literature from Proust to Malraux.

My enthusiasm for Paris did not diminish my affection for Berlin. My friends and I knew that we were very fortunate to be able to live in Berlin in the twenties. Certainly Berlin was not a particularly beautiful city: it had no great palaces or historical monuments, and, with the exception of a few neo-classical buildings from the early nineteenth century, most of its houses were modern and many displayed a showy vulgarity. But Berlin was surrounded by lakes that mirrored in their waters the tall, slim spruce trees of the Mark Brandenburg. Berlin's broader streets were framed by large chestnut and linden trees, and it had a wonderful climate—not too hot in summer, invigoratingly cold in the winter.

Most of all, however, Berlin was an intellectually exciting city. Its isolation from the outside world, first during the war and then in the years that immediately followed, created a restless eagerness to catch up with what had been going on elsewhere, and to make Berlin a center of new movements in art, music, and literature. Berlin in the twenties was emphatically "international," and foreign visitors of distinction were eagerly welcomed. I heard Arnold Toynbee, Johan Huizinga, and Rabindranath Tagore speak at the university, and I remember seeing André Gide sitting in the center box at a commemorative celebration for Rilke. From the first half of the nineteenth century Berlin had always been a capital of musical life; I doubt, however, that its musical offerings had ever been as brilliant as they were in the twenties. Berlin had three large opera houses, all for the staging of serious operas, and one placed special emphasis on modern operas and experimental productions. Three outstanding conductors directed the orchestras at these operas and the Philharmonic concerts: Wilhelm Furtwängler, Bruno Walter, and Otto Klemperer. Although in later years I had some reservations about Furtwängler's interpretations, during these years his conducting

of Beethoven's symphonies was unsurpassed and unsurpass-
ble. The greatest concert I can remember was in the enor-
mous, overcrowded Philharmonic Hall, with Casals sitting
very small and lonely on the immense stage playing nothing
but Bach the entire evening.

Yet Berlin's best offerings during these years were the theater
performances; and they were the chief topic of many conversations. During the winters no week passed without my going
at least once to the theater. When at the end of the month
my budget was exhausted and I could not afford a seat, it was
"standing room." I doubt that any city has ever had as many
theaters playing simultaneously as Berlin did in the 1920s.
There were three state theaters, four theaters under the direction of Max Reinhardt, a similar number under Victor Bar-
nowsky, and many other theaters for serious plays and social
comedies.

In reminiscing about the Berlin theater of these years, I
must begin with the name of an actress about whom all Berlin was crazy, and I no less than anyone else: Elisabeth Bergner. I believe I saw her in every play in which she appeared
during these years, even in a role in which she appeared no
more than four or five times because the production—*La Dame
aux Camélias*—was a failure. Elisabeth Bergner was not only
the graceful and charming heroine of Shakespeare's comedies,
or the childlike *Joan of Arc* of Shaw, but a great interpreter
of difficult psychological roles such as those in Strindberg's
tragedies or O'Neill's *Strange Interlude.* However, Elisabeth
Bergner was not the only great actress on the Berlin stage in
the 1920s. The list reaches from Maria Orska in Frank
Wedekind's plays, full of sex without passion, from Tilla
Durieux in Shaw's *Pygmalion,* from Helene Thimig as an Austrian aristocrat in Hofmannsthal's *Der Schwierige,* to Marlene
Dietrich stepping down a broad staircase in tuxedo and top
hat. However, if the acting was admirable, the manner of
production was no less a cause of excitement. Max Reinhardt

was *the* great producer of the time, and in his gigantic play-house—a circus transformed into a theater—he staged, one evening a serious, strictly stylized *Oedipus,* and another evening Offenbach's comic opera *Orpheus in the Underworld,* bubbling with contemporary allusions. Other producers dared to present Shakespeare or Schiller in stark, bare settings and costumes, so that all attention would be directed to the words, their content and meaning. In consequence, we added to the canon of classics our own classics: Heinrich von Kleist's *Penthesilea* and Georg Büchner's *Danton's Death.*

The theater in Berlin was profoundly exciting not only because it was frequently great art, but also because it was intensely political. It was no longer an expressionist outcry against all social conventions, which it had been immediately after the revolution of 1917, but it was still a manifestation against old traditions, a place for social criticism and for denouncing restrictions of freedom. Not only did modern plays—those by Ernst Toller, Georg Kaiser, and Carl Zuckmayer, the most admired of the young poets—serve these purposes, but so did older plays like Schiller's *Don Carlos* and Hauptmann's *Weber.* Brilliantly produced and acted, these suddenly seemed to be written for our time and for us. The greatest and most unforgettable production, however, in which art and politics was beautifully combined, was Brecht and Weill's *Threepenny Opera,* which played before full houses for years and which I must have seen three or four times. It gave a grim, hopeless picture of a world in which corruption controlled human life and society. Yet it had a fairy-tale ending: the mounted messenger of the king arrives at the last moment, saving the hero from execution.

In my description of Berlin in the twenties I have given a picture of the life, or at least of the thinking, of people who felt more and more the approach of an evil power, and the unavoidability of the collapse of the world in which they had set their hopes. What is misleading in this, and what I have been unable to depict, is that whatever we rationally thought about the future, we never gave up hope that the mounted messenger of the king would arrive.

Chapter IV

Friends of School and Student Days

THE FOLLOWING biographical sketches of a few of my friends from school and student days are meant to throw additional light on my life in Berlin before the Nazis came to power. The number of these biographical sketches is small. The friends about whom I write are no longer alive. As long as a friend is alive, you don't have, and don't want to have, the distance required for a summing up. Only after the death of a person close to you will you try to assemble your memories into a picture that remains. Moreover, I have included only those friends who were born within a year of my own birth. When the Nazis came to power, each generation in Germany faced a different situation. Those of us born around 1905 were at the beginning of our professional careers, and we had to decide whether we wanted to continue and whether we could continue, with what we had intended to do. These sketches ought to be a reminder that what I shall report about my life in later chapters is not unique, but only an example of what happened to a generation.

WOLF VON TROTHA

I WONDER whether this account of my first great friendship is more imaginary than real. I saw Wolf von Trotha frequently and regularly only during the three years from 1911 to 1913, when we both were six to eight years old. We went to the same preparatory school, and almost from the first day on were inseparable. After school in the afternoons Wölffchen, as he was called by me and everybody else, came to my house and we played together. Nevertheless, the next morning at school, we were as happy to see each other again as if we had been separated for a long time. In my memory Wölffchen was a remarkably graceful and sweet boy, and this cannot have been entirely wrong because once when we were playing together at our house I heard a friend of my mother ask: "Who is this beautiful boy with whom Felix is playing?"

Wölffchen's blond hair was cut off in a straight line along the front and the sides so that it seemed like a helmet placed on his delicate oval face. He was always amiable. I don't think we ever had a fight, or even a loud exchange of words. Our school was coeducational, and, of course, we admired the same girl. We walked her home from school, one on her right side, the other on her left, the one confirming and underlining what the other said.

Wölffchen's father was a naval officer, and in 1913 he was transferred from Berlin to Kiel, the main harbor of the German navy. It had been agreed that Wölffchen would visit me during the next school vacation, but a few days before his expected arrival I received a postcard: his parents had decided he ought not to leave Kiel so soon. I still remember reading the postcard, standing in a corridor that opened into a room with a large window; suddenly it seemed no light came into that room, and the entire world had become dark. There was nothing to look forward to any longer. Even now I find it painful to think back to this moment. Of course, this was not the worst blow I have ever received: it was the first time, however, that I felt utterly alone. I was absolutely sure that nobody could understand my feelings or help me.

I saw Wölffchen again after the war. His father had been retired from the navy, and the family had moved back to Berlin. We were still good friends, but our meetings became less frequent; we lived in different parts of the city and went to different schools. Moreover, there were many things we could not talk about any longer. The circles in which our families moved were quite different, and so were their political views. Wölffchen's father, embittered about the end of the war and his retirement, was extremely nationalistic. Later I noticed that Wölffchen's younger brother had become a leading man on the staff of the Nazi ideologue Alfred Rosenberg. Before his family left Berlin again Wölffchen and I lost contact with each other.

In the 1950s, while working in the Reading Room of the British Museum in London, I discovered that the genealogical handbook of the German nobility had resumed publication, and that its volumes stood on the shelves. I immediately reached for the volume that contained the genealogy of the von Trotha family, and there I read, "Wolf Heinrich Otto Alexander von Trotha, born Kiel, April 18, 1905, killed east of Taganrog, July 20, 1944, colonel and commander of the First Armored Regiment."

DIETRICH BONHOEFFER

SO MUCH has been written about Dietrich Bonhoeffer that it may seem superfluous, almost presumptuous, to add to these writings, especially since my acquaintance with Dietrich was sporadic, and his theological concerns rather distant to me. Yet he was a person about whom one cannot hear enough, and in justification of the following I might add that I suspect that there are very few people still alive who knew Dietrich as I did, as a young boy.

We were both students at the Friedrichs Werdersche Gymnasium and were in the same grade, although not in the same section of this grade. The two sections took a few lessons together, however, and Dietrich and I had many opportunities to talk to each other. My sister was then, and remained throughout her life, a close friend of Dietrich's eldest sister, and together with my sister I had visited the Bonhoeffer house and had known Dietrich even before we became students at the same Gymnasium. Of course, I cannot remember what we talked about, and it was hardly of any importance. What I remember now most clearly from those days is Dietrich in a snowball fight. He was then taller than most of us, and rather sturdy; he was blond and blue-eyed, the impression of blondness perhaps strengthened by the fact that his fair hair stuck out from under a dark fur cap. He was standing on a wall of snow, tossing the snowballs with great accuracy. Although his team had no formal leader, it was quite obvious that he was its leader. The team I was on soon gave up.

The Bonhoeffers moved away from Berlin's western section into the Grunewald, but for a while we continued to meet quite frequently. Near the house where the Bonhoeffers lived was a swimming pool that Dietrich frequented and where I took swimming lessons. He gave me additional instruction after my lessons had ended and, if my memory is correct, was quite a strict taskmaster. We both began to study in the spring of 1923, Dietrich in Tübingen, I in Heidelberg. We had agreed that he would visit me in Heidelberg, but in the end the visit did not come off.

From that time on until about 1933 we saw little of each

other. During the second half of the 1920s we both studied at Berlin University, but our fields of study were very different and we never took the same courses or attended the same seminars. Moreover, I had received many reports about how amazingly well Dietrich was doing in his studies, which he completed in a remarkably short time, and I felt somewhat overawed by this kind of perfection. I had also heard that while studying in Tübingen Dietrich had received military training in the Black Reichswehr—so-called because this temporary training of young men for military service was forbidden by the Treaty of Versailles—and I suspected that our lives were developing along rather different lines.

An accidental meeting either in 1931 or 1932 showed me that I had jumped to wrong conclusions. I was riding a bus from the western suburbs to the university. It was a pleasant day, and I climbed up the stairs to the open upper deck. When I sat down on the bench and looked at the person next to me, it was Dietrich. We immediately engaged in a lively conversation. He had just come back from the United States and talked with great enthusiasm about his visit. He had been particularly impressed by the interest he had found among American religious groups in the need for international understanding and the maintenance of peace. In this respect the social atmosphere in the States seemed to him better than in Europe. We found that we were in agreement in our desperation about the unemployment crisis, about the human tragedy it involved and the lack of energy displayed by the Brüning government in tackling it. The unemployment problem seemed to us to make irrelevant the solution of other political issues the Brüning government had put in the foreground—whether it was the *Anschluss* or rearmament. It was now clear to me where Dietrich would stand if the Nazis came to power.

After this bus ride I saw Dietrich again only outside Germany, in London and New York. I knew, of course, that in

October 1933 he had moved to London to be a minister in one of the six German churches there. I had emigrated to London at about the same time, and on one of the Advent Sundays of 1933 my sister and I went to the church where Dietrich was preaching. Dietrich and I then arranged that I would visit him from time to time in the evenings. He was very busy and frequently absent from London, and early in 1935 he returned to Germany. I don't know any longer how frequently I made the trip to his vicarage in a south London suburb, but I remember one visit very clearly. Dietrich had to leave the room shortly after I had arrived, and I picked up a pamphlet lying on the table. It contained a sermon by Martin Niemöller, a leader of the opposition to the German church of the Nazis. On its cover was a photograph of Niemöller in the uniform of a German submarine commander. I said to myself, but evidently loudly: "Terrible," and Dietrich, who was just coming back into the room and had heard my remark, said, "Yes, it is terrible that in order to be heard you must now appear in uniform."

Although Dietrich was much absorbed with the affairs of his German parish in London, my impression was that he felt somewhat lonely, separated from his principal concern: the struggle, which was then just beginning, against the integration of the church into the Nazi regime. Dietrich and I talked about the extent to which the church should be actively involved in the problems of social and political life, or whether it ought to be concerned with such issues only if its mission was threatened by external forces. Dietrich could hardly have expected that I had much to contribute to this issue about which he knew immeasurably more than I did. But I think our discussion showed how concerned he was, during these months in London, with thinking out his position. Moreover, to a certain extent Dietrich was interested in discussing ideas because of what they revealed about the human being with whom he discussed them. At the forefront of his thought

and actions were the individual human being and the human
community.

I left England for America in 1936, and Dietrich and I
met again in New York in the summer of 1939. I had a small
apartment in Greenwich Village, and one morning I got a
telephone call from Dietrich who was giving a summer course
at the Union Theological Seminary. We arranged for an evening on which Dietrich would visit me, and it became a long
evening. He arrived in the afternoon and stayed until late at
night. Then we walked together a good stretch of the way
toward Columbia University, until finally we entered a sub-
way station and took trains in opposite directions. I was leaving the next day for a weekend in Connecticut, and we agreed
that we would get together again after I returned. When I
telephoned after my return, I was told that Dietrich had left
for Europe.

I realize that I had little chance of persuading him to stay
in the United States, but I was unhappy that because of my
trip to Connecticut I had not been able to see him again
before his departure and to make a final attempt. Dietrich
mentions our meeting in his diary, where he writes that he
learned from me about Roosevelt; I cannot remember our
discussing this subject, but it seems likely that I tried to
explain to him that although Roosevelt detested the Nazi
regime, there were restrictions on his actions. We certainly
discussed politics. We were both sure that war would break
out soon, and a main subject of our discussion was whether
Dietrich should stay in the United States and accept a position that had been offered to him. Actually, his published
papers show that he had made his decision a few days before
we met. But as he himself says, it was a somewhat intuitive
decision, and when he talked to me about this issue, he probably wanted to test the extent to which it stood up to rational
considerations.

Dietrich gave me two reasons why he believed he ought to

return to Germany. "The Brethren" were one reason: he was engaged in forming a group of young ministers ("brethren") who would struggle against Nazi encroachments. The preservation of a true Evangelical church in Nazi Germany depended, Dietrich believed, on the continued existence of such a group. The other reason he gave me can be found in a published letter to Reinhold Niebuhr: "I will have no right to participate in the reconstruction of Christian life in Germany after the war if I do not share the trials of this time with my people." What he said to me was somewhat more general: if he remained away from Germany he would not be able to play a role in the rebuilding of the country after the war. The difference is slight but, I think, throws some light on what seemed to me a very essential and very moving element in Dietrich's attitude. There was no personal ambition in his wish to have a role in Germany after the war. Dietrich was not a political person in the sense of being concerned with the introduction or the reestablishment of particular institutions, or with the construction of social utopias. He had very close ties to his family, his friends and colleagues, the people among whom he lived; he saw *them* behind the institutions, and his overwhelming urge was to help save for them the possibility of a meaningful life. Would he be heard if he separated his fate from theirs?

When, in his diary, Dietrich writes about our New York meeting, he refers to our common schooldays. When I think of Dietrich, my first memory is that of a boy full of life, leading his comrades in a snowball fight. Friendships of early boyhood create impressions that remain.

LOTHAR PREUSS AND ERICH WRESCHNER

THE Friedrichs Werdersche Gymnasium, which I attended from 1916 to 1923, was one of the oldest humanistic Gymnasiums in Berlin. Originally in the center of town, it had been moved to a new building near the Tiergarten on the northern side of the Spree. During my first years in the Gymnasium, if the weather was all right I usually walked through the Tiergarten—about thirty-five minutes each way—to and from school, frequently in the company of Hans-Werner von Brandenstein, with whom I had also been together in preparatory school. But the Brandensteins left Berlin after the 1918 revolution, and then my closest friends in the Gymnasium were Lothar Preuss and Erich Wreschner.

Both were Jewish, which aroused no particular attention in our school; if anyone was teased and tormented, it was the son of a Protestant minister, a virtuous grind who in addition had the Germanic name of Volkmar. Neither I nor anyone else in my Gymnasium found the fact that three or four students in our grade were Jewish in any way worth commenting on. Certainly I have read in many books and articles about the steadily rising wave of anti-Semitism during the years of the Weimar Republic. On the basis of personal experience I cannot subscribe to such a view. There was a wave of anti-Semitism in the early twenties, and then again, of course, in the years just before the Nazis came to power. Otherwise there was open anti-Semitism in Catholic Bavaria, and a covert anti-Semitism in academic circles and "high society." I don't think, however, that during the twenties anti-Semitism gained strength and became more widespread and more virulent. If one spoke of Jewish doctors and Christian doctors, the main difference was that Christian doctors were often connected with a university, whereas Jewish doctors usually had private practices. The distinction pointed to the actual conditions in which they performed their professional duties, rather than implied a value judgment.

Lothar Preuss was the son of a widow of rather restricted means, Erich Wreschner the eldest son of a well-to-do owner of a textile business. Originally I was closer to Lothar than to

Erich. I played chess with Lothar, we went regularly to the theater together, and during the last two school years we took lessons in Hebrew twice a week, between seven and eight in the morning. At the time I was thinking of studying Arabic, and for this it would have been useful to take the Hebraicum, the examination—given either at the university or at the Gymnasium—that was a precondition for the study of theology. Moreover, having Jewish ancestors it seemed to me that I ought to know more about the Jewish past, and Lothar, who I believe had never gone to the religious lessons rabbis gave to Jewish students in the Gymnasium, felt the same concern. We both passed the Hebraicum in our last year of the Gymnasium. Erich and I became friendly because we sat next to each other in school, and during our lessons whispered to each other disrespectful remarks about our teachers, whom—with one or two exceptions—we considered to be reactionary Philistines. Lothar, Erich, and I founded a kind of literary club, because in our lessons in German literature we did not get beyond Goethe and Schiller; actually our literary circle itself was rather tame because in our readings and discussions we did not venture much beyond Ibsen, Strindberg, and Hauptmann.

For their vacations Lothar and Erich had stayed in resorts relatively close to Berlin, on the Baltic Sea or in the Harz Mountains. I was surprised, therefore, when Erich told me that he intended to begin his law studies in Heidelberg. We decided to travel to Heidelberg together. My mother and Erich's parents said good-bye to us at the railroad station; the solemn farewell on the platform seemed to Erich and me rather unnecessary because we could not understand why they should be apprehensive about their "adult" sons (Erich was just eighteen and I was still seventeen) embarking on an independent life.

I—or, more correctly, my mother—had arranged for my housing in the Neuenheimer Landstrasse: a lady living in a

large apartment on the third floor of an old house along the
Neckar—only two houses removed from the house where Max
Weber had lived—let rooms to students. Two days after we
arrived in Heidelberg Erich came to me in desperation, saying that his housing was intolerable. I had noticed that a
room was free in the apartment in which I was renting a
room, and so Erich moved in. Thus he became part of my
Heidelberg semester, and I of his.

We went to the theater in Darmstadt together, and traveled to Frankfurt to attend the celebration in honor of the
National Assembly that had met there seventy-five years before
in the Church of St. Paul. I introduced him to the beauty
and luxury of Baden-Baden. We bicycled along the Neckar
and took walking tours in the mountains. He told me about
the law lectures he attended and I told him about my history
and philosophy courses, and together we went to the sociol-
ogy lectures of Alfred Weber. For Erich this was the discovery
of a new world. Before our semester together in Heidelberg I
had not realized how little he knew of Germany outside Berlin and the areas near it. Nor did I know that the social group
in which his parents moved consisted almost exclusively of
quite prosperous middle-class business people whose interests
focused on what was going on in Berlin. It was quite evident
and moving to observe how his horizons were widening.
Another student with a room in our apartment was a young
lady from the Rhineland, and when she and Erich fell in love
with each other—very innocently, I would say now—his
transformation was complete.

After the semester in Heidelberg Erich continued his studies in Berlin, where Lothar also was studying law. Although
we saw each other less and less, we kept in touch. I knew
that Lothar was planning to become a lawyer. Erich wanted
to become a judge (the study of law in Germany could lead
either to the practice of law or to a position in the adminis-

tration of justice), and he was certainly well suited to such a career.

The three of us were in closer touch again after 1933. Lothar was immediately dismissed from his clerkship and went to Breslau to train for a job in the business of a cousin of his. He then—partly because he was unhappy in this job but also because he was aware of the steadily deteriorating prospects of Jews in Nazi Germany—went to an agricultural school to prepare for emigration to Palestine. I discussed with Erich at length what he ought to do, but I could not persuade him to leave Germany. He worked in the business of his father, who needed him, and continued to believe that Jews would be able to remain active in business; he did not want to leave Germany. When he finally realized that he had to leave, it was too late. Erich died in a Nazi extermination camp.

In 1971 I visited Israel; I had been invited to give lectures in Jerusalem and Haifa. One morning I got a telephone call from Tel Aviv. It was Lothar Preuss, who had read about my lecture in a newspaper and wanted to see me. I said that unfortunately I was leaving that same day for Haifa, where I would stay for only two days before sailing to Istanbul. Lothar said he would come to Haifa. After greeting each other somewhat shyly—unsure of how the other had fared in the intervening forty years—Lothar reached into his briefcase and produced a perfectly preserved photograph of our class at the Friedrichs Werdersche Gymnasium. As in any other class photograph, tall boys stood in the back row, and the rest of us were arranged by decreasing size. With our hair neatly combed and suitably serious expressions on our faces, we all looked so much alike: well-educated, well-behaved boys with a promising future. Like any two classmates thumbing through a school yearbook, we could point to a face and almost always recall the first name; when one of us did not remember the last name, the other could supply it. We knew that some of our classmates had been killed in the war; others were victims of the Holocaust.

We sat on the hotel veranda looking down on Haifa and the sea—a universe away from the day the photograph was taken at the Friedrichs Werdersche Gymnasium. Lothar had married and had grown-up children, but it was clear that he had had a very hard life. We both immensely enjoyed seeing each other again, but it was a strange meeting: in the short time at our disposal, it was impossible to recount all we had experienced in the intervening years. Again and again we fell back on reminding each other of this or that incident from our Gymnasium days, assuring each other that despite the gaps created by the years of living in other parts of the globe, there was still common ground.

THEODOR E. MOMMSEN

IN THE 1950s, a short time after I got married, Theodor Mommsen visited us for a few days in Bryn Mawr. In his thank-you letter to my wife he reminded her that she had called him Ted, and indeed this was how he was addressed in the United States; but his old German friends called him Theodor, and since her husband was his oldest and best German friend, he would like it if she too called him Theodor. Although this remark was intended simply to establish a close relationship with my wife, it touched upon a very personal problem that accompanied Theodor throughout his life.

Since our families knew each other and we were even distantly related, it seems there was never a time when I didn't know Theodor. His parents told me once that they had gotten engaged at a party in my grandmother's house. Theodor and I attended different Gymnasiums, but we were "confirmed" in the same church and after that we were together a good deal. In 1922 Theodor spent the summer vacation with my family in the house my grandmother had rented in Rindbach. It was a very enjoyable summer; but there were days when for hours Theodor hardly spoke and clearly preferred to be by himself. Later I became aware that, from time to time, he had his depressive moods. Soon after he began to study he told me that he preferred to be called Theodor E. Mommsen— not Theodor Mommsen, as he had been christened. This concern with his name was an indication of a deep and troubling issue: as the grandson of the renowned ancient historian Theodor Mommsen, he was heir to a great scholarly tradition, but this legacy was a heavy burden.

He tried hard to fend off those who measured him by the standards established by the work of his grandfather, and could be devastatingly sharp in rejecting such comparisons. One of his school companions told me that after Theodor had made a mistake in a translation from the Latin his teacher shouted at him, "Your grandfather would turn round in his grave." Theodor replied very quietly: "You told me that once before, so he must now lie on his back again."

Such remarks certainly did not endear him to his teachers. Still, what happened in his last school year has to be attributed to Theodor's wish to demonstrate that he was not a second Mommsen, rather than to the malevolence of his teachers. Theodor and I had agreed that after we passed our final examinations we would begin to study in Heidelberg in the spring of 1923. To my great surprise, however, a few months before our planned departure, Theodor told me that his teachers would not allow him to take his final examinations in the spring and that he would have to remain in school another half year. At that time final examinations in a German Gymnasium—the *Abitur*—were not so difficult that a person of Theodor's intelligence could not have managed to pass them; rather, he had let things slide to make it obvious that he was not a reborn scholarly genius.

The struggle to free himself from family tradition and to become a person in his own right was unusually difficult because of the surroundings in which Theodor had grown up. His father, a well-known medical doctor, had inherited the house in which old Theodor Mommsen had lived. One of the rooms was dominated by a Lenbach portrait of old Mommsen: it was a remarkable painting, but also frightening because it depicted the formidable, inhuman absorption of a great scholar in his work. The pursuit of scholarship was most highly esteemed in the Mommsen household, and Theodor alone among his brothers and sisters had the talent and inclination for scholarly work. His parents provided him most liberally with the means to pursue whatever academic studies attracted him. But with this support came the pressure to become as great a scholar as his grandfather had been.

I should add that Theodor's mother's maiden name was Weber. The burden of high expectation on Theodor was not lightened since in addition to being a grandson of Theodor Mommsen, Theodor was also a nephew of Max Weber. When in the fall of 1923 Theodor began to study at Heidelberg (I had by then left) he lived in the house of Marianne Weber, Max Weber's widow, and became even more aware of this heritage.

After a year in Heidelberg Theodor returned to Berlin and told me that he had decided to study Chinese history. I was horrified, in part because the decision implied that we would be eating frequently in Chinese restaurants, which in Berlin were terrible and the cause of my everlasting dislike of Chinese cooking. But there were more serious reasons for my disapproval of Theodor's decision. It did not seem to me rooted in a passionate concern with China or interest in the Chinese; it was an effort to move his academic pursuits as far as possible away from the fields in which the great men of his family had excelled.

It was foreseeable that Theodor would not remain permanently in Chinese studies, and, indeed, he abandoned them before two years had passed. The time he devoted to this field was, however, valuable. He spent a few months in Paris working with Chinese language experts there and then went to the University of Vienna to study with one of the foremost German scholars in Chinese history. In Paris he fell in love with modern art, and in Vienna he became interested in modern psychology. During these years he acquired a deep and lasting interest in twentieth-century art and literature, and in the modern world in general.

These were not the usual interests of a historian working in the field on which he finally settled: medieval history. His friends—I among them—urged him to study modern history, but he considered the modern field overcrowded, as indeed it was in Germany in the 1920s, when war and revolution turned the attention of most younger German historians to the study of recent events. Moreover, the concern with modern history seemed to Theodor to contain an element of trendiness he did not like—an attitude that, to a certain extent, reflected the scholarly values that were part of his family tradition.

When Theodor decided on medieval history, the field in Germany was dominated by the Monumenta Germaniae Historica, a research institution founded in the last century for the purpose of editing and publishing medieval sources. During the nineteenth century, the Monumenta had developed into a model of scholarship in its most organized and institutionalized form; in the twentieth century under Paul Kehr, who knew how to get along with emperors, popes, and Prussian socialist ministers, the Monumenta dominated the field of medieval studies more than ever before. In the years when Theodor and I studied history, there had developed among younger scholars a resistance to the prevailing emphasis on editing and publishing sources at the expense of interpretation, although too much criticism of the historical establishment was hardly advisable for those aiming at a scholarly career in medieval history. Ernst Kantorowicz's work on

Emperor Frederick II, which was published in 1927, demonstrated that a different kind of medieval history, one that revealed the ideas and values that motivated the rulers of the Middle Ages, was possible and might have a wide appeal. Even if one did not share the political and literary views and values of Kantorowicz, who was a member of the elitist circle around the poet Stefan George, one admired his book for overcoming the rigidification that had set in in medieval history because of an overemphasis on historical techniques. After completing his Ph.D., Theodor almost immediately became an assistant in the Monumenta Germaniae and one of Paul Kehr's great favorites. But Theodor was also a great friend of Kantorowicz, whom he had come to know when Kantorowicz was working in the Berlin libraries on the second volume of his *Frederick II*. Theodor's friendship with Eka (as Kantorowicz was called) lasted throughout his life, and became particularly close during Theodor's later years when both of them resided in Princeton, Theodor a professor at the university, Eka a professor at the Institute for Advanced Study.

For Theodor, working for Kehr and friendship with Kantorowicz did not solve the problem of the extent to which nineteenth-century scholarly values and attitudes were still valid and had to be maintained. Nevertheless, for several years Theodor's work did not require him to take a stand, and these issues remained in the background. As an assistant in the Monumenta he was charged with the collection of documentary material on the activities of the German kings in Italy during the fourteenth century. Although his headquarters was the German Historical Institute in Rome, Theodor spent much of his time traveling in Italy and visiting archives, even in the small towns. He told an amusing story about one of these visits. He had announced by letter to the director of the archives of a small Italian town that he would arrive at a certain day and time to take a look at one of their documents. When he descended from the train he was faced by a group of gentlemen dressed very formally in black. The mayor of the town, two members of the town council, and the director of the archives all had come to receive him, and greeted him with a lengthy oration. Of course it was Theodor's grandfather whom they had expected to welcome, and it took some time, much tact, and polite maneuvering to explain the true situation without hurting anyone's feelings.

In Italy the memory of old Theodor Mommsen was no less alive, and perhaps even more so, than in Berlin. Once when Theodor and I were both in Florence I introduced Theodor to Robert Davidsohn, the author of the magisterial *History of Florence;* I was slightly annoyed when Davidsohn concentrated exclusively on Theodor and I was condemned to the role of a silent onlooker. Later Theodor lived for some weeks in Davidsohn's house, and in his last will Davidsohn handed over to Theodor his papers so that he might continue and complete Davidsohn's lifework, *The History of Florence.* I suspect that Theodor's entry into another famous house in Florence, Bernard Berenson's I Tatti, was smoothed by the famous name he bore; Theodor became a frequent visitor there. Even Hermann Göring, who visited Rome in 1933, and to whom Theodor was introduced at the Prussian Historical Institute, could not refrain from referring to old Mommsen: "The German people will always be grateful to your grandfather for his words about the decomposing spirit of Judaism." (Göring referred to a somewhat unfortunate formulation of old Mommsen in a writing in which he actually attacked anti-Semitism.)

Theodor regarded his scholarly legacy as a burden and an obligation. He quite frequently said: "I am not a book man; I am an essay man"—a remark that was not only factual but contained a value judgment as well. He believed a real scholar ought to be a book man. Despite his awareness that different times required different scholarly aims, the multi-volume work and the large documentary publications remained for him the manifestation of true scholarship. Throughout his life Theodor had an unjustifiably low opinion of his own work, and as one of his colleagues wrote in Theodor's obituary: "To him his work lacked unity, authority and volume. . . . He was judging by the standards his grandfather had set; he had in mind the army of major works usually associated with the name Mommsen."

It was obvious that Theodor could not live in Nazi Germany. Some members of his family ascribed Theodor's decision to leave Germany to the fact that his best friends—the classicist Ludwig Edelstein and myself—had left, but this is nonsense. Theodor was much too skeptical, too perspicacious, and most of all too distrustful of authority to be able to exist under Nazi rule. It was fortunate that he was not yet teaching at a university when the Nazis came to power because he could leave Germany without arousing much attention, which would have been damaging to some members of his family. Paul Kehr acted with great understanding and tact. He entrusted Theodor with research tasks in Italy as long as possible, but since assistantships at the Monumenta were of limited duration, he finally had to tell Theodor—I believe it was in 1935—that he could no longer keep him as an assistant working outside Germany. Theodor now had to decide whether he wanted to go back to Germany to teach at a university or look for an academic position in another country.

Although to Theodor and his friends it was evident that he could not live in Nazi Germany, it remained a very hard decision. Whereas others who left Germany emigrated with their families or, at least, some members of their families, for Theodor it meant separation from his family. His father had died, but his mother, two brothers, and two sisters all remained in Germany. Moreover, in Germany he had a recognized place among the younger group of German medievalists.

However, for Theodor, coming to the United States also

had its favorable aspects. What had been a serious problem for him in Germany—the conflict between traditionalism and new approaches in historical method—receded into the background. The kind of archival research the work in the Monumenta had required was not possible in the United States. So in the United States Theodor worked on historical issues that, while connected with the research he had done for the Monumenta, had then been on the fringes of his interest. He wrote on Petrarch, and he began to work on what became, in my opinion, one of his finest articles: an analysis of the historiographical concepts of the church fathers Orosius and Augustine (now included in *Medieval and Renaissance Studies,* a collection of his essays published after his death). Theodor arrived in the United States with a fellowship at Johns Hopkins University; he then became an instructor at Yale, and when Yale did not want to keep an enemy alien during the war years, he taught at Groton, where he had a most happy time; there he could do scholarly work out of his love for scholarship rather than as a professional duty. He was pleased, however, to return to a center of scholarly life when he was appointed to Princeton in 1946. There he had many close friends, especially among the younger historians. He had an apartment in the same house as the art historian Bert Friend, with whom he discussed problems of medieval history almost daily; Ernst Kantorowicz's coming to Princeton closed the circle. After the war Lenbach's portrait of old Mommsen, which had been left to Theodor, arrived in the United States and hung, forbidding and dominating, in Theodor's living room.

Theodor seemed so much at home in Princeton that he astonished many people when he left and went to Cornell. Alluding to what he had said to me twenty-five years before, when I had tried to persuade him to go into modern history, he said to me jokingly: "In Princeton there are too many competitors in medieval history." Although this was hardly a reason for his move, it was important to Theodor that at Cornell he would be the main professor in his field. He enjoyed being able to teach the entire field of medieval history because he firmly believed in its unity; he did not like to see medieval history taught in distinct chronological or regional sections. For Theodor the notions on which medieval studies had been founded in nineteenth-century Germany remained valid, and he certainly believed that the medieval period ought to be explored by the techniques and methods that had been in use since the nineteenth century. Despite his reservations about the influence of the Monumenta, he believed that some training in its methods would be good for graduate students, and he sent some of his Cornell students to Munich where the Monumenta had been reestablished after the war. Theodor seemed happier at Cornell than ever before, and in the summer of 1958 the news that he had ended his life came to me not only as a sad shock but as a complete surprise.

Afterward I talked about Theodor's suicide with his brother Konrad, who had always remained in contact with him, had visited him in Princeton and Ithaca after the war, and who was also a good friend of mine. We both agreed that in previous years when, as it happened from time to time, Theodor was in a depressive mood, we had sometimes worried about what he would do to himself. But in his last two or three years we both had the impression that this danger no longer existed.

Theodor had visited us in Bryn Mawr perhaps a week before his death. He had a terrible cold and was depressed; he had just been to Baltimore where he had said farewell to the dying wife of his friend Ludwig Edelstein. He spoke enthusiastically, however, about the coming academic year, when he would be on leave and would be able to spend some time in Germany, where his mother, brothers, and sisters still lived. He seemed to be very much looking forward to a year in Europe. I ought to have been aware of the dangers inherent in such plans, of the disquieting and upsetting aspects of a lengthy stay in Germany. Since 1935, Theodor had visited Germany only very briefly in 1948, with the sole purpose of seeing his nearest relations. In 1958 he was planning to stay there for most of the year which would mean reentering the German world. For many of those who had left Nazi Germany, the possibility of living, if only temporarily, among its people aroused strong and ambiguous feelings. This I knew, but it should have been clear to me that it was a particularly dangerous step for Theodor: he would return to Germany as a man whose political attitude had been fully justified, and as a recognized scholar. But at the same time, the German surroundings would reawaken his feelings of not coming up to the expectations his name aroused. I am quite sure that this was a difficult problem for him throughout his life; whether it played a decisive role in his suicide I don't know. There was nothing among his papers that provided an explanation.

HEINZ HOLLDACK

HEINZ HOLLDACK was tall and slim, carefully, even elegantly dressed, with a white handkerchief in his breast pocket and a monocle in his left eye. Women of every age found him attractive, and he was certainly attracted by quite a number of them. When I first met him in the historical seminar of the University of Berlin, I decided on the basis of his appearance that he must be an arrogant snob and I decided not to like him. We attended a few seminars together, and I gradually had to admit that he was unusually quick and perceptive. After we had some conversations and I got to know him better, I, like others, found him charming and highly amusing. Of the stories he told, my favorite was about his experiences in the Reichswehr. After passing the final examination of the Gymnasium he intended to become an army officer,

and entered military service as an officer's candidate. As such
he was permitted to subscribe to two newspapers; he selected
the *Frankfurter Zeitung,* then the leading German democratic
paper, and *Le Temps,* then the leading French newspaper.
Holldack was called before his commanding officer, who
explained to him that there were complaints about the newspapers he wanted to subscribe to. Holldack assumed that it
was the subscription to a French newspaper that had met
with disapproval, and explained that even if you did not
approve of French policy, it seemed useful to know what the
French were thinking. The officer replied: *"Le Temps, Le Temps,*
who cares about *Le Temps?* But does it have to be the *Frankfurter Zeitung?"* This story is an example of the spirit of the
military during the period of the Weimar Republic. But it
is also characteristic of Holldack: he was a person of great
independence, unwilling to accept opinions because they were
the prevailing views in the circles in which he moved.

At the University of Berlin he had chosen Erich Marcks as
his teacher. Next to Meinecke, Marcks was the leading historian in Berlin, and the official biographer of Bismarck. If
Meinecke attracted the students of left-wing inclinations,
Marcks attracted mainly right-wing students. Once Holldack
attended a party in Marcks' house; also present were Walter
Frank, who later became the head of the Federal Institute for
Contemporary History under the Nazis, and other aspiring
historians of a similar extremist political outlook. At one point
Marcks commented: "We can speak here frankly; we are all
on the same side," to which Holldack said "Oh, no, I am
republican and socialist." I have been told—secondhand, I
admit—that in this circle Holldack's remark had the effect
of a bombshell. To be fair to Marcks, it ought to be said that
this incident did not change the high opinion he had of
Holldack as a promising historian.

As Holldack and I came to realize that we had scholarly
interests and political concerns in common, we began to see

more and more of each other. We started work on our dissertations at the same time, and showed each other what we had done. Often in the evenings we met to discuss and criticize each other's work. Such meetings were usually followed late at night by conversations in some bar about the problems of the world, and we would part in the early mornings after having strengthened ourselves at a street corner stand with a roll and coffee.

We both finished our dissertations and passed our final examinations in the winter semester of 1929–30. We decided to spend the summer in Florence, where I would work on the origin of the idea of balance of power and Holldack could do research on the reforms of the grand duke Leopold of Tuscany, an enlightened despot. Free from the pressures of writing a dissertation and final examinations, we enjoyed the summer of 1930 immensely. We rented a small cottage on the road from San Domenico up to Fiesole, from which we had a view of Florence with the tower of the Signoria and the cupola of the Duomo. Most mornings we took the streetcar down to Florence, looking out over the landscape and also avidly reading the *Frankfurter Zeitung,* which was then publishing installments of Hemingway's *Farewell to Arms.* Many evenings we stayed in Florence until late at night, sitting in a café on the Piazza Vittorio Emanuele; we then took the streetcar to San Domenico and walked from there to our cottage, partly on the road, partly through vineyards, with the beautiful, gentle lines of the hills surrounding Florence clearly visible in the dark blue night.

The summer passed quickly, and we had our amusing experiences. The study room in the Florentine archives was very small (all this has been changed), with two tables for students in the middle. On one of our first visits to the archives one table was crowded, and so we sat down at the empty one. Almost at once an employee of the archives appeared and told us to move to the crowded table. We had sat down at the table reserved for ladies, and ladies and gentlemen were not allowed to sit at the same table in the archives. During a visit to Ravenna I said to Holldack on the second or third day, "I have now spent all the money I took along, you'd better pay from now on," and he replied: "I didn't take any money along." By selling Holldack's walking stick, which had a silver handle, we managed to settle our hotel account and avoid being put in prison.

We had many visitors in our cottage: Holldack's brother, who was a medical student, my friend Theodor Mommsen, another friend of mine, Erich Jacoby, who was a trade union lawyer, and finally Eugen Dollmann, whom I had come to know while studying in Munich. He visited us shortly after the September election of 1930, which had brought the Nazis their first great increase in votes. We composed a satirical play imagining all the awful unimaginable things that would happen if the Nazis came to power—which, despite the elections, seemed quite unlikely. A few years later Dollmann became the SS colonel in Rome, and I have always regretted losing the manuscript of our play and being unable to send it to Himmler.

Holldack and I returned to Berlin in October 1930. From then on, until the spring of 1933, I lived part of the time in Berlin, where I was preparing my dissertation for publication and editing the political writings of Droysen for the Prussian Academy, and part of the time in Italy, working in the Florentine archives and in the Prussian Historical Institute in Rome. Holldack also moved between Germany and Italy, but spent more time in Italy than I did. The reason was that he was thinking of changing his profession and becoming a journalist. As I have mentioned, events in Germany raised certain doubts about the chances for an academic career for a person of leftist leanings. Since Holldack was not very enthusiastic about fitting himself into the strict patterns and demands of academic life, especially since, as the son of a professor, he was very much aware of what these demands were and implied. Eckart Peterich, then the representative in Rome of a large chain of German newspapers was a friend of Holldack's. Peterich offered Holldack work in his office as a voluntary assistant, so that if Peterich left Rome Holldack could take over. This is what actually happened; in 1933 Peterich left Rome for Berlin and Holldack became his successor.

Holldack's journalistic activities created new possibilities for the pursuit of an interest we had both shared and that had intrigued us since our first days in Florence: how did Fascism really work, and how oppressive was the Fascist regime? Tourists visiting Italy were not very much bothered by this issue, but it posed very serious questions for those who stayed in Italy for a greater length of time and had political interests.

Outwardly the Fascist regime in Italy had glamor and seemed popular. Soon after Holldack and I had settled in Fiesole it was announced that Mussolini was coming to Florence and would speak from the balcony of the Palazzo della Signoria. We decided to go. When we left the streetcar in the center of town, throngs of people filled the narrow streets issuing into the Piazza della Signoria. Caught up in the crowds, we could barely move forward. There seemed no chance to get near enough to see the Duce. Italians are wise people, however, and do not like to stand in the sun. A small triangle of ground that was not covered by the shade of the palazzi surrounding the piazza was almost empty; risking the danger of a sunstroke, we took our stand there close to the Palazzo della Signoria. Mussolini appeared on the balcony directly above us and began to speak. The speech was a famous political manifesto directed against France, declaring the Mediterranean an Italian sea. At the time our attention was absorbed by the technique of Mussolini's oratory. His voice changed from loud to soft, from fast to slow; he was like a conductor directing an orchestra. It seemed that on his command the

people shouted or were silent, expressed indignation or
applauded, and, like the finale of a symphony, the speech
culminated in a great ovation on the part of the audience.
From a purely rhetorical point of view, it was a magnificent
performance.

We learned quickly, however, that in Fascist Italy there
was not much reality behind the rhetoric and appearances.
Sometime later Holldack, then a journalist, was invited to be
present as the Duce inaugurated the rebirth of Tarquinia, a
town in the Pontine swamps that, because of malaria, had
been abandoned. It was said that through Fascist efforts the
swamps had been drained and the town made fit for habita-
tion. Holldack asked me to accompany him. We had been in
Tarquinia for half an hour when Mussolini arrived, surrounded by Blackshirts. He made a short speech, and then
walked along the main street of the little town, inspecting
the houses, being photographed, and posing with the inhabitants who gave him lively signs of their gratitude. Then
Mussolini, with his cohort and a crowd of newspaper people,
drove back to Rome. Holldack and I decided to stay on and
observe the ordinary life in Tarquinia. It was afternoon, the
sun was setting, and almost immediately the streets emptied,
the doors of the houses were closed, the windows were shut
and locked. The inhabitants knew only too well that the mos-
quitoes were still at work and that the Fascist claim of having
regained this area was false.

In the years that have passed since Holldack and I were in
Italy we have experienced so much cruelty, arbitrariness, and
oppression that the cases of supervision and coercion we
observed during the late twenties and early thirties in Italy
now seem minor and hardly worth mentioning. Yet for me
Italy was a great demonstration of the indignities involved in
living in a dictatorial regime, of the impossibility of compromise with such a system.

A few incidents made this clear to me. When at a dinner

at Robert Davidsohn's, the conversation turned to politics, Davidsohn suddenly put a finger to his lips and ordered us to be silent: the Italian maidservant had entered the room. Another time a friend of Benedetto Croce had given us a recommendation to Guido de Ruggiero, professor at the University of Rome and author of a famous history of liberalism. After attending his lecture at the university we presented him with our letter of recommendation. He looked at it for a second and said quickly: "In my apartment this afternoon at three o'clock"; clearly he did not want to be seen in conversation with foreigners. Yet another time in a small restaurant we had frequently seen—and exchanged a few words with—two young Italians. Suddenly they no longer appeared. When we inquired, it emerged that one evening they had made some critical remarks about Mussolini. The next day they were taken to prison, and as long as we were around they did not reappear. In Fiesole we had frequently talked to a middle-aged man who seemed a most loyal adherent of the regime. One day we met him in Florence and, talking about money, he exploded: "If he [Mussolini] had a mountain of gold he would eat it up" ("Se avesse una montagna d'oro mangerebbe anch'essa"). Only away from Fiesole, from those eager to denounce him, did he feel on safe enough ground to say what he really thought.

Like myself, Holldack could have no illusions about what would happen in Germany when the Nazis came to power. Yet he did not want to give up the position he held: from the time that we were together in Fiesole, he declared that Italy was where he wanted to live, and he saw no other way of fulfilling this desire than to keep his position as a German journalist. I disapproved of his decision, and our relations lapsed when I left first for England and then for the United States.

After the war was over we came into contact again. I had heard that throughout the war years he had kept his distance from the Nazis. Indeed, after the war he became editor of the *Süddeutsche Zeitung,* and he then entered the diplomatic service of the German Federal Republic: he served in the embassy in Paris, then was consul in Naples, and finally became head of the cultural section of the German embassy in Rome. There we met again—more than twenty-five years after we had been together in Fiesole. We were sitting together in a restaurant on the Piazza Navona, not in the elegant Tre Scaline but in a cheaper restaurant from which we looked out on Borromini's enchanting—both floating and solid—facade of St. Agnese. I asked him: "And what did you really do in the Nazi time?" I had hardly opened my mouth when I was aware of the stupidity of this question. Both of us were historians, and I knew the answer I would receive—the famous answer Sieyès had given when faced with a similar question: "I kept alive."

Chapter V

The Rise of the Nazis to Power

IN THE summer of 1932 I went to Italy to work in the archives on Renaissance history, and I stayed until June 1933. For the Christmas Holidays I returned to Berlin. Schleicher had by then succeeded Papen as chancellor, and although many had doubts about Schleicher's politics and personality, it was clear that his government offered the last chance of keeping the Nazis out of power. But the shakiness of Schleicher's position was very evident by the end of 1932. On the train back to Rome I read in the newspapers about a meeting between Papen and Hitler that had taken place on January 4, 1933, and I feared that the struggle was over and lost. Indeed, on January 30 the evening papers in Rome announced that Hitler had been appointed chancellor.

It is difficult to describe the following months. In most respects life went on as before, and I have some pleasant memories of that winter and spring. The winter was unusually cold, and on the mountains around Rome there was snow, which brought to mind Horace's "Vides ut alta stet nive candidum Soracte"; friends of mine, the Dohrns, and I decided to climb the snow-covered Soracte. It was a shivery expedition, and we were glad to find a hut on our way: an open fire gave off some heat, and the simple interior of the hut, which was inhabited by people who spoke with an incomprehensible accent, seemed to indicate that nothing had changed there since Horace's times.

During these months I wrote a few brief reports on literary and cultural events in Italy for the *Frankfurter Zeitung;* in pursuit of this task I attended the opening of an exhibition of the works of a young sculptor, Marino Marini, and was delighted to meet there—and talk at some length with—a young writer, Alberto Moravia. His first novel, *Gli Indifferenti,* had come out shortly before, and I had read it with great admiration. At Easter time Rome was as usual thronged with tourists, among them several German acquaintances; on the night of the day of the Crucifixion, songs of lament could be heard in Rome's darkened churches, and on Easter Sunday I stood in the crowd waiting for the Pope's appearance on the balcony of St. Peter's. Nevertheless, thoughts about what was happening in Germany were ever present. I followed events in the newspapers, but learned most through letters I received from friends and relations. Some of them, written to me in Rome and Florence, are published in this chapter: they throw some light on the astounding and terrifying developments in the course of which the Germans became obedient instruments of an incredibly brutal, totalitarian dictatorship.

In publishing these letters, I have omitted some passages of purely personal interest, although I have left a few remarks of this sort standing because it would be wrong to give the impression that the world was exclusively concerned with politics during these months. A few of the letters were written by members of my family: my grandmother, Enole Mendelssohn Bartholdy; an aunt, Edith Mendelssohn Bartholdy; and my sister, Mary Enole Gilbert (called Mämi in the family).

My aunt, whose husband, as I have reported before, had served as an officer *(Rittmeister)* in the German army and had been killed in the First World War, lived in Leipzig. Since 1918, she had been active in politics as a member of the German Democratic Party, and for several years had been elected to the municipal parliament of Leipzig. In 1933 she was the director of a gallery she had founded that exhibited popular artworks and handicrafts produced by the people living in the mountains of Saxony and Bohemia. The gallery had been financed by a Jewish banker, had aroused much attention, and had been quite a success. My aunt left for England in the later thirties, but after the war returned to Germany where she had her own radio program, which focussed on the problems of the elderly.

My sister lived in London in 1933; she had studied German literature and received her doctorate from the University of Berlin, and had also studied in Frankfurt, where she passed the state examination giving her the right to teach at German high schools (Gymnasiums). Her minor field was English, and in the fall of 1932 she went as an exchange teacher to London. She gave instruction in German, but did this mainly to perfect her English, which, to my great envy, became so perfect indeed that hardly anyone realized that it was not her native language. Until her death in 1976, she continued to teach German literature at the University of London, first at Bedford College, then at Queen Mary College (which during the war was evacuated to Cambridge), and finally at King's College.

The other letters were written by friends of my school and university years, most of whom I have mentioned previously. All these letters express strong disapproval of the Nazi regime, perhaps with varying degrees of vehemence and decisiveness,

except the letter of R. W., which reveals a somewhat different outlook. It seemed to me appropriate to publish this letter from a young, twenty-one year old history student whom
I had met in the course of my studies, because it shows that
Nazism was not only an aberration but also a seduction, and
that the strength and attraction of the movement was not
unknown even to those who, like myself, lived in a circle of
decidedly anti-Nazi people. Readers will notice that only very
gradually did the correspondents became aware of the existence of censorship, and that then the letters frequently assume
an ironical tone, praising what the writer actually detests.

Although it might appear in retrospect that with Hitler's
appointment on January 30, 1933, the Weimar Republic had
ended and been replaced by a totalitarian dictatorship, these
letters make clear that, despite the rapidity with which
democracy was destroyed, it nevertheless was a gradual process. It might be well, therefore, to mention quickly the
most important events and measures of the following months
by which the Nazis solidified their power and embarked on
the realization of their program.

Hitler's appointment to the chancellorship was connected
to a dissolution of the Reichstag and the calling of new elections, which were to take place on March 5, 1933. Before
they were held an emergency decree was issued on February
4 that strictly limited the freedom of the press and the right
of assembly. Then, on February 27, a fire destroyed the
Reichstag, which the Nazi leaders immediately blamed on
the Communists. On the following day, February 28, another
emergency decree was issued that more or less abolished the
basic rights of the individual and stiffened the punishment
for any action that might be considered directed against the
well-being of the Reich. The elections on March 5 made the
National Socialists by far the largest party in the Reichstag,
but did not give them a majority; that could be attained only
in combination with the German National Party (Deutsch-

Nationale), and even that combination was not sufficient to make up the two-thirds majority needed to change the constitution. With the support of the Catholic Center Party, however, on March 23, the National Socialists achieved the two-thirds majority needed to pass an Enabling Act which gave the federal government the right to enact laws, even laws that contravened the constitution.

From that time on, resistance to the Nazis and their measures no longer had any legal basis. The two most noticeable demonstrations of government-protected violence and brutality were the boycott of Jewish shops and businesses on April 1, and the burning of the books on May 12. Yet these were only the most visible manifestations of a process that had been set into motion. On April 7 parliamentary state governments ceased to exist when a law was passed that entrusted rule in the various German states to a *Reichsstatthalter* (commissioner) appointed by the federal government. On the same day, the law for the restoration of the professional civil service was issued; by this law all civil servants who without appropriate qualification had been appointed since November 1918 were dismissed, as were civil servants of doubtful loyalty to the Nazi regime; non-Aryan civil servants were retired. Since university professors in Germany are civil servants, in accordance with this law there began the dismissal of a large number of professors for political as well as racial reasons. On May 1 the SA and SS occupied the offices and buildings of the trade unions, and a united labor front under Nazi leadership was formed. A change in leadership was forced on the organization of large industry (Reichsverband der Industrie) to make them "conform" *(gleichschalten)* to the new regime. Even in the less important industrial organizations, new leaders were installed and Jewish businessmen were excluded from participation in these associations; they were replaced by men of pro-Nazi sympathies. If in February and March the Hitler government had focused mainly on establishing itself securely in the political sphere, from April on it concentrated on extending its power into education and business administration. The impact of Nazi control on the lives of individuals became more strongly felt, and the thoroughness with which the Nazis aimed to carry out their program became more evident.

During these months it was still by no means clear how far the Nazis would go in their anti-Jewish policy, and whether Jews would be excluded not only from the administration, the civil service, and leading positions in public organizations, but also from any activity in economic life. Until the Nuremberg laws of 1935, it was uncertain what restrictions would be placed on people like my sister and myself who were, according to Nazi categories, twenty-five percent Jewish. But from the beginning it was evident that pursuit of an academic career in Nazi Germany was impossible, and that life under this regime would be unbearable. The Jewish policy of the Nazis was entirely in accord with the brutal and barbarian system they established in Germany. To say, as I have heard some say in Germany, and more in Great Britain and the United States, that the Nazi regime would have been bearable, or even acceptable, were it not for their anti-Jewish policy seemed to me from the outset, and seems to me now, nothing but a sign of political shortsightedness and stupidity.

1. *from* HEINZ HOLLDACK

Dresden, February 8, 1933

You're absolutely right. I should have written you about politics. You would have favored undertaking an action if you had had any influence. Why now? After the failure to mobilize the forces of the Prussian state in response to the breach of the Prussian constitution last fall,[1] only the trade unions are left, and they can do nothing because the federal government has still not given sufficient ground for action, that is, for a general strike. All we can hope for now is that before the elections a sufficient number of brutalities, also in the area of constitutional law, will occur. You are much mistaken when you assume that people have put their excitement on ice. It grows every day, and it's a pity that election day does not come later. For the time being the "entanglement" with Hugenberg is the best thing we can have,[2] for any economic measure—and at the moment all we have are plans for a moratorium on agricultural debts—enacted by this government is bound to be highly unpopular and will kick back at Hitler. Hugenberg is a liability to Hitler. Only after the election, of course, will Hugenberg finally reveal the full extent of his plans. . . . conflict with the unions will then certainly follow. I spoke here with Schulze's brother,[3] a union lawyer from Berlin, who knew Jacoby, Kehr, Holborn, and others. I told him that in my view a general strike under the present economic conditions and with six million unemployed was unthinkable. But he was optimistic; he thought that the prospects were not hopeless and the unions intended to strike after the elections if need be.

Fear seems to be making the Communists gradually back away from their ideological tactics of indirectly favoring Hit-

---

[1] In 1932 the German federal government under Papen had declared martial law and removed Prussia's Socialist prime minister Braun and his government from power; Braun's government appealed to the federal supreme court in Leipzig against this violation of the Prussian constitution, but did not use its forces, chiefly its police, against the measures of the Papen government.

[2] Hugenberg, the conservative leader of the German National Party (DNVP), had become minister for economics and agriculture in the Hitler government; he was close to the leaders of heavy industry.

[3] Schulze was a journalist working at the same newspaper as Holldack. The names that follow are those of friends with whom Holldack and I studied in Berlin, and who we were sure would be hostile to the Nazis.

ler.[4] In the Saxon parliament they have always voted for motions of no confidence directed against the rather conservative Schinck government composed of civil servants. Yesterday they helped Schinck win a grand victory when the National Socialists, German People's Party, and German National Party moved a vote of no confidence.

It is obvious that you are personally depressed by the events. My fundamental impression is that the reign of law is beginning to totter and that for the moment at least, the centuries-old European tendency toward even greater freedom has come to a halt on German soil. And on top of that is the horrifying stupidity and hollowness, the crudeness and brutality of this petit-bourgeois vindictiveness that has taken over the reins of government. It is all utterly disgusting, and when you open the newspaper, you get sick to your stomach. The *Aufruf* was bad enough to read. But if you had heard it on the radio . . .[5]

II. *from* MY SISTER

London, February 15, 1933

I'm in a situation similar to yours: completely despondent about German politics and just as completely flabbergasted by how unperturbed people are about it, according to the letters I'm getting. It is extremely embarrassing when everyone assumes that I should know where we are heading. Everybody from my housekeeper to all the teachers and students on up to Lady Cripps[6] has asked me: What about Hitler? And I find the choice between the truth and "my country

[4]Communists and National Socialists had cooperated in various strikes, particularly the Berlin strike of public transport workers of November 1932.
[5]On the evening of February 1st, 1933, the day after his appointment to the chancellorship, Hitler read over the radio a very rhetorical appeal *(Aufruf)* to the German people, stressing conservative, Christian, and anti-Communist views.
[6]Lady Cripps was the wife of Sir Stafford Cripps; they were friends of my sister.

right or wrong" rather *difficult*. Most of the time people here are so "nice" as to ask naively: "Do you love Hitler?" And the greatest fuss is being made over the return of the kaiser, about whom there was a truly marvelous cartoon in the *Daily Mail*. The only extensive report I've had was from Haase,[7] in answer to a request of mine. I think I'll look around for another job here for the fall!

III. *from* MY GRANDMOTHER

Berlin, February 15, 1933

Did you hear Hitler's speech![8]—It was enough to make you explode with annoyance and fury. It was a genuine miracle that he didn't explode himself with all his bellowing.— The future is disquieting—but I have the feeling that by and large people here are accepting all this rather calmly—they are probably getting hardened with all these events, one following on the heels of another.

IV. *from* THEODOR E. MOMMSEN

Berlin, February 18, 1933

More than two weeks have gone by since I received your letter, but this time I have a legitimate excuse. I had the flu early in the month, and though it did not last long it left me horrendously tired and lethargic.

I can't say that my mood is very good. We're living under pressure, and that takes some getting used to, doesn't it? So I try to have a good time, go to what is for me a lot of dances and other social gatherings, go frequently to the movies. A lot of people seem to be experiencing this need for amusement. I understand that all "public entertainments" are bet-

[7] My friend, Arnold Haase.
[8] On February 10 Hitler had opened the election campaign with a speech in the Berlin Sport Palast.

ter attended than ever. But when you see in the Esplanade[9] members of society of the ancien régime with von Papen at their head and among them the leaders of the Berlin SA, Counts von Helldorf and von Arnim dancing in brown uniforms with swastika armbands and knee-high boots, then you have seen demonstrated *ad oculos* the fondest dream of this same Mr. von P.—the union of good old conservative elements with those of the awakening masses, these "people," symbolized by their noble, brown leaders—but can this substructure hold up in the long run?

For the time being everything is going along smoothly, if we ignore the interpretations of the constitution à la C. Schmitt,[10] which are not worthy of further mention. They are hardly of importance any longer. We're in a state of latent revolution; the crisis will come soon. The people in government are already in quiet strife, and it won't be long before the fight breaks out in the open. The game of the little man from Westphalia[11] who thought it would be easy to lead a camel with a halter will soon be up. I spoke with Holldack about this. He thinks "they"[12] would gladly let others take care of the actual business because they themselves have no one and nothing. I don't believe that. There's no doubt that they want all the power, not just a share of it, and just as certainly they believe they can supply the necessary people for doing the job of governing. But it is really pointless to write about these things. We mustn't give words to what we really think and fear because it's too horrible to even imagine. It's best to keep to oneself now or spend time with people who don't matter to you. It's completely impossible to speak about things with so-called "good friends." No "discussion"

[9] One of Berlin's most elegant hotels.
[10] Carl Schmitt, the German political scientist who defended the Papen government against the Socialist Prussian government before the federal court in Leipzig; in 1933 he was a defender of Nazi totalitarianism.
[11] An allusion to Papen, who owned estates in Westphalia.
[12] The Nazis.

can take place anymore, given this horrible division that has so split us apart that one can hardly speak of being one nation any longer. That, no doubt, is precisely why people in the government talk about the nation so much.

V. *from* HEINZ HOLLDACK

Berlin, February 19, 1933

I saw Marcks recently.[13] It was very interesting from the point of view of politics. He himself knows the Old Gentleman.[14] I'll give you a detailed report some other time. He confirmed the impressions I have from reading the *D.A.Z.*[15] and the *Börsenzeitung*. He's furious about the Old Gentleman and particularly about his son.[16] The son is "stupid and rude." Of course, one[17] wanted full dictatorial powers for Schleicher: antiparliamentarianism, but cooperation with the unions. And for that reason anger also about Hugenberg. Marcks says (get this!): A general strike is perhaps necessary. If there were rioting, the Reichswehr would act in a nonpartisan way. I'm afraid this is seen too much in Schleicher's perspective. Michael,[18] Marcks says, has pulled away from Schleicher and is very Christian, but politically on ice. That is a small personal plaster on very large public wounds.

Life here is very bitter, my friend. There is no point in writing about the personal disappointments you have to swallow. I shall tell you about it.

[13] Erich Marcks, professor of history at the University of Berlin, had been Holldack's teacher. Well known as a biographer of Bismarck, Marcks was conservative and monarchist. His son, an official in the Reichswehr, had been close to Schleicher and, when Schleicher was chancellor, had been chief of the Press Section and one of Schleicher's most influential collaborators.

[14] Hindenburg.

[15] *Deutsche Allgemeine Zeitung*, a right-wing newspaper, but not Nazi.

[16] Oskar von Hindenburg, son and adjutant of the *Reichspräsident*.

[17] Schleicher and his group.

[18] Horst Michael, a historian a few years older than Holldack and I, was politically right wing and had played a role in the Schleicher government. He had then broken his ties with Schleicher but had not been fully accepted by the Nazis.

VI. *from* HEINZ HOLLDACK TO ECKART PETERICH[19]

Dresden, February 28, 1933

The political situation in Germany is gradually becoming so bad that I yearn for the day (Sunday, the fifth) when I'll be able to put this country and its barbaric people behind me. You probably can't even imagine how extensive the personal terrorism is already. The uniformed bandits come into your apartment and ask what newspapers you subscribe to; they go into the cafés and collect money and everyone gives because he is afraid. It makes for depressing studies on the cowardice of humankind. I had some interesting conversations in Berlin. As in everything, of course, the people there are in still greater despair than in other German states because, thanks to the government by Commissars,[20] the feeling of absolute legal insecurity is much greater. I was told in Berlin that even now there is open conflict between the "German Nationals" and the Nazis in the cabinet and that the German Nationals can't do anything. And despite all this, Herr Hugenberg still hasn't come out with his decisive economic measures. Blomberg and Hammerstein[21] were described as very reasonable people who, if the chips were down, would

[19] Holldack had gone to Germany to get instructions from the directors of the newspaper concern whose correspondent in Rome he was to be. In Rome he was succeeding Eckart Peterich, who was moved from Rome to Berlin. This letter by Holldack was sent to Peterich in order to inform him about the German situation in preparation for Peterich's move to Berlin. But Holldack knew that Peterich saw me frequently and that the letter would be shown to me.

[20] Since Papen had removed Prussia's Socialist government, Prussia was ruled by a government of "Commissars." When the Hitler government was formed, although Papen was officially at the head of the Commissars' government, Göring and the Nazis actually wielded power.

[21] Blomberg was minister of defense in the Hitler government; Kurt von Hammerstein was army chief.

turn the army loose even on the Nazis. People in Berlin once again regard the possibility of a general strike as very dangerous because feeling among the workers is running so high that acts of sabotage might be committed. Then the police and possibly the army would have to be sent in against the workers, and the SS and the SA, of course, would then stand side by side with the troops and the police. In Berlin I was told that the restoration of the monarchy would be the last hope. I couldn't believe my ears; some people actually want to bring William back. And in the south, Rupprecht.[22] Saxony would be incorporated into Prussia. The Social Democrats are prepared to swallow the monarchy for fear of Hitler. I pointed out that in North Germany, at least, the monarchy seemed to offer no guarantee against Hitler, because I couldn't see what interest the monarch would have in ruling against Hitler. If Hitler guarantees him the throne, then Hitler would make the best monarchal chancellor. I left Berlin with the feeling that I'd been talking with people who had completely lost their heads. The next morning Schulze, with whom I discussed these matters, gave me a confidential report from Bahr,[23] which contained the very things I had been hearing the day before. In the afternoon in the dance hall of the Europahof in Dresden I saw a picture of Friedrich August framed in the white and green flag.[24] Bahr reported some very comical details: people in Berlin are starting to pay visits to the Netherland Palais,[25] where Hermine has taken up residence again. I think this is all madness, whatever the concrete foundation of such projects might be. There are still two possi-

---

[22] Eldest son of the last king of Bavaria.

[23] A journalist in the newspaper concern in which Holldack and Peterich worked.

[24] Green and white were the colors of Saxony; Friedrich August was the last king of Saxony.

[25] Netherland Palais was the name of one of the Hohenzollern castles in Berlin, where the second wife of William II, Hermine, stayed when she came to Berlin.

bilities one can resort to, before fetching back that idiot from
Dohrn.[26] 1. The Old Gentleman and the German Nationals
get furious. Then, on the basis of an almost certain vote of
no confidence in the Reichstag, they can boot Hitler out, and
with the support of the army they can govern dictatorially
without and against Hitler. 2. The Old Gentleman forces
Hitler to form a coalition with the Center . . . I think the
Center would join such a coalition. By and large, this possibility seems now the most desirable solution to people in
Germany. Personally I don't think much of it because I can't
really see how the Center could control Hitler. I'm not as
nervous as the people in Berlin about the prospects of a new
presidential election, for I think that the Communists, after
the bitter experience they are having right now with their
insane policy of terror (today Reichstag),[27] would support a
Social Democratic candidate in the second vote. If the Communist Party is proscribed, nothing will prevent their people
from voting for the Socialist candidate. Till then we have to
let the Nazis do their part and, with threats from the Old
Gentleman and the army in the background, prevent them
from committing acts of extreme violence. Then we can put
them down by force. My thinking has, however, two weak
points. 1. What happens if the Communist Party should be
proscribed before May 3?[28] The inevitable result would be a
right-wing majority in the Reichstag. I don't know what the
position of the Supreme Court in the case of a proscription of
the party would be, but I fear on the basis of material available it would let the proscription stand. It's impossible to say

[26] William II.

[27] The Reichstag fire had taken place the day before this letter was written; it is
interesting that before the Nazi propaganda had made full use of this event, it was
not considered a milestone.

[28] He means before the opening of the newly elected Reichstag. This is what happened. Voting for the Communists was permitted, and eighty-one Communist
deputies were elected, but their seats were declared invalid immediately after the
election.

what would happen with a right-wing majority in power. 2. It can be said that I'm letting too much depend on the Old Gentleman. But that's only the way things appear to people abroad who simply can't conceive of the existence of palace governments in the twentieth century anymore. You probably have to be a historian to understand that. My teacher Marcks, who knows the Old Gentleman quite well, says that he has slipped badly in the last year and is completely under the influence of his "son, who is not provided for in the constitution." This son is "stupid and rude" and so unpredictable that you can't know what bright ideas he'll come up with next. From these negative statements of a Hindenburgian you now have to subtract the resentment that Schleicher's followers are feeling about the Old Gentleman's "breach of loyalty." Schleicher, by the way, seems to have overcome surprisingly well his leukemia and is dreaming of a putsch with Gregor Strasser.[29] Sic transit gloria mundi! . . .

I'd like to ask Gilbert and Dohrn not to send me any more postcards with pictures of camels on them and the caption "The new German government." We are not in Italy, the land of free speech, where Croce and Cappa are allowed to write books.[30] Up to now, I haven't had to reproach myself for personal cowardice, but I prefer not to get such postcards.

VII. *from* MY SISTER

London March 6, 1933

I can't think about Germany at all. If I do, I turn green with rage and anger, and nobody else reacts that way. I think everybody in Germany has completely lost their wits. Thea[31]

---

[29] A National Socialist who had defected from Hitler in December 1932.

[30] Benedetto Croce, the famous philosopher and historian, and Paolo Cappa, a well-known writer; both were able to publish in Italy, despite their avowal of opposition to the Fascist regime.

[31] A cousin of ours.

wrote me a very reasonable letter but was of course pleased
about Hugenberg and fully convinced that he is the stronger.
Ursel[32] wrote that Rüdiger is favorably impressed with the
competent people in his office and that it is necessary to vote
German National to prevent chaos. . . . Primitive as I may
be, I find the election results at least clear—did Papen think
of this back in January? I wish him all the worst. What I
can't figure out is how the middle classes voted. The German
Nationals didn't win, nor did the Center, nor the SPD.[33]
And where did the Communists' vote go? Only now are people here starting to feel uneasy. A reliable source told me
yesterday that in France the word among the students is:
Why study for exams? We'll be at war by summer. I'm so
outraged over the dismissal of civil servants, the Karsen
school,[34] the Academy,[35] prohibition of books, vice squads,
and sanctimoniousness. What I find so awful is that I don't
have any idea what the mood really is, whether it seethes or
whether everyone is just delighted. I'll be looking around for
a job here, because I can't teach Nazi children; I find that
entirely senseless.

VIII. *from* ARNOLD HAASE

Berlin, March 11, 1933

. . . Events here are coming thick and fast. What we
thought impossible yesterday is reality today, and we have
clearly to understand that Germany is undergoing a right-

[32] Ursula Schleicher, born Bonhoeffer; her husband, Rüdiger, was an official in
Göring's Air Ministry. In 1945 he was executed because of his participation in the
conspiracy against Hitler.
[33] Social Demokratische Partei Deutschlands (Socialists).
[34] Fritz Karsen was an influential advocate of modern pedagogical ideas who had
founded and organized a school that the Nazis closed.
[35] The process of purging the civil service had been going on since February, although
the relevant law (Gesetz zur Wiederherstellung des Berufsbeamtentums) was issued
only on April 7. Heinrich Mann had been removed as president of the Writers'
Academy.

wing revolution at the moment, with all its consequences. It is utterly astounding how calmly and routinely life in Germany goes on. The reports of the incidents that have occurred have probably been somewhat exaggerated abroad. These incidents are attendant circumstances to this revolution, and I am not inclined to attribute any serious implications to them. Still the situation is very serious, and we all hope that these present developments will not endanger Germany's position in the world. There is no point in writing more about these things. You know the reason for this.[36]

I'm really looking forward—finally, after almost a year and a half—to the prospect of a vacation and a chance to speak with you in peace and in detail about these things of such importance to us.

IX. *from* EDITH MENDELSSOHN BARTHOLDY

Leipzig, March 12, 1933

I can hardly find the courage to write—what I'd like to say I can't, and to report about personal matters seems trivial and irrelevant. Who would ever have thought things would come to this sorry pass in our supposedly enlightened nation? We're in the same boat as the Italians: we have to keep our mouths shut and grit our teeth. I'm often glad that you are not here, but on the other hand I don't know whether it mightn't be important for you, from a purely scholarly and professional point of view, to experience all this. I do know, however, that you would suffer a great deal. Is that any less the case if you are far away? Things often look a lot worse from a distance than they do up close. I can't accurately assess how you regard things and what effect they're having on you.

[36] The reasons, of course, were the existence of mail supervision and control. The entire letter is ironic.

In any case, being here is altogether dreadful. I watched as some workmen, under police supervision, took down the German flags at the market with a huge mob of people present. The police then "confiscated" the black, red, and gold flag and raised the swastika flags everywhere. We all have had to experience and endure so much since 1914, that we can only hope that this bitter cup too will pass from our poor country. But by the time it does, mightn't culture and even civilization be completely lost? If I only could, I would pull up stakes and head south. . . . But it doesn't look as if one could go there ever again.

X . *from* R . W .

Issy les Moulineaux, March 13, 1933
I've been meaning for a long time to write you a detailed report about my studies here. In the meantime, everything I have wanted to tell you and ask you has piled up so high that this will probably become a long-winded scribble. I hope you'll manage to put up with it.

First of all: our beloved homeland! Because this letter will presumably go by way of free Switzerland, I can chat away here safe from all possible snoopers. That does not seem to be such a sure thing with the Paris-Berlin mail anymore. This last week has bought us a national "victory" over all the state governments and what seems to be an altogether obvious waning in Hindenburg's personal resistance to the Nazis.[37] For me personally, it is extremely important to be living here just now; for if I were at home, I would probably be drawn into some hopeless form of opposition. What seems to me more and more decisive as an explanation for the German reaction, as well as a cause for our present economic troubles,

[37] On March 9 the Bavarian government, under the Catholic prime minister Held, had been deposed and the pro-Nazi general Franz Epp had been installed by the federal government as *Statthalter* (federal commissioner).

is this instinctive, almost animal-like egotism of the otherwise so civilized French, an egotism that automatically condemns any other form of national life and that strikes me here time and again with frightful clarity in discussions that aim at a true understanding of things rather than the defense of opposing positions. Especially here, and in contrast to this delightful slovenliness I find so profoundly sympathetic, in contrast to this disorderly, excitable, French bliss that Sieburg worships but that is unfortunately so egotistical and narrow-minded—under these circumstances it seems to me more and more essential, as Sieburg[38] once remarked, to steer Germany's development toward the political realization of what is probably the only fruitful concept to come out of the world war, namely, that of comradeship. And isn't it natural that the world war generation, now that half the years we reckon to be a generation have passed since the end of the war, wants to give one of its most profound experiences concrete form in the life of the state? German thoroughness has made this process take longer with us than it did in Russia and Italy, but for that very reason it may perhaps become more European and humane and in the end more democratic as well. But just as it is impossible for me to curse our country in these times and become a "Frenchman," which many people have done inwardly and which is not particularly difficult to do because virtually anyone, whether Negro, Chinese, or Canadian, can become a "Frenchman" if he is willing to genuflect before the indisputable superiority of French civilization—it is equally impossible for me to do what so many of our dear fellow citizens are doing, which is, within twenty four hours, simply to forget the history and the men of the fourteen postwar years, men who have pulled Germany out of the swamp the Hohenzollerns left behind them. Furthermore, despite

[38] Otto Sieburg, who had been the correspondent of the *Frankfurter Zeitung* in Paris, was the author of one of the great literary successes of these years, a book on France entitled *Gott in Frankreich* (God in France).

my best efforts at understanding, Hitler's personality and that
of some of his comrades from the Munich putsch evoke nothing but the most extreme skepticism in me. As they constantly point out themselves, the national awakening is
reminiscent—suspiciously so—of the hysteria of 1914, and
now that we have happily lost the Russians in Geneva, we
can only hope that the end of the disarmament conference
will not turn out to be a frightful debacle of our foreign policy.[39] I hope you will be good enough to forgive me this
outpouring of highfalutin generalities, but I can assure you
that continuing discussions with these French who are so fab-
ulously intelligent and who are always in the right force you
either into constant combativeness or that genuflexion, which
I cannot perform in political discussions without committing
inner suicide. As Andre Siegfried once said, I prefer the continuous European discussion to French self-glorification, which
is reminiscent of American or Russian monotony . . .

XI. *from* ARNOLD HAASE

[Berlin], March 21, 1933

The chances of my getting away from here as planned on
the Thursday before Good Friday look good. I'll wire you at
the end of this week so that you can reserve a room
for me.

I would have to write a letter of many pages if I wanted to
report at length about things in Germany.[40] You will be
informed about details from the newspapers. It is generally
welcomed that at long last we have ousted the foreign elements from the administration, the legal system, and busi-

---

[39] The Russians in the preceding months had taken a more positive attitude at the
disarmament conference in Geneva toward the proposals made by Great Britain,
the USA, and also France—proposals Germany opposed.

[40] This letter, of course, is ironic; it shows—like most of the following letters—
the increasing awareness and fear of Nazi censorship and control.

ness—or at least significantly reduced their numbers. I can pass on to you the gratifying news, for example, that the Jewish influence has been largely eliminated in the important industrial and commercial associations too. Now we can set about pursuing a national economic policy free from those practical and personal scruples of the past. . . .

XII. *from* MY SISTER

London, March 26, 1933

Mrs. Nauheim—who has just returned[41]—has begged me to tell you to refrain from judgments and to be more cautious in your letters. Your last had been opened, and it could become very unpleasant for everyone involved.—I have to admit that I have heard the same request from all sides.

XIII. *from* ERICH WRESCHNER

Berlin, April 7, 1933

Many thanks for your card. I hadn't the faintest idea that you had chosen the city of the Seven Hills as your residence. Or have you gone there only temporarily because of the Anno Santo? The way things are looking now I don't think I'll be able to manage a visit with you. At any rate, I would be pleased no end if, as you suggest, the possibility of direct communication via one of your friends should open up. Please let me know if someone comes to visit you.

Lothar's and my situation is in keeping with the circumstances. In purely physical respects we have no reason to complain. In every other, things do not look so rosy. You will know from the papers that there are no longer any Jewish judges on the bench in Prussia. The same can be said for all the other professions as far as official positions are concerned.

[41] From Germany.

In addition, Jewish notaries have been forbidden to conduct any official business. Except in very few instances, Jewish lawyers may not appear in court or before other government agencies. The same measures are in the making for other professions. It makes no difference whether artists, doctors, businessmen, etc., are concerned.

Beyond that I can't tell you any more or anything different from what you can read in the papers.

At the moment it is impossible either to make plans for the future or foresee further developments because the national revolution is still not brought to a close and because each day can bring new surprises.

In my humble opinion the most important challenge this government of national concentration will have to face is to overcome the economic crisis and the connected question of unemployment. I do not have any detailed information on how these problems can be solved. But it is certain that the government will soon have to tackle the issue of economic "recovery."

It's very easy for me to put myself in your shoes when you write that you can't really imagine how things are here. There are many people whose imaginations are failing, even though they live this side of the Brenner Pass and have experienced the events of recent weeks and months *intra muros.*

Do you have any clear plans for your near and distant future? Will you be kissing your native soil in the foreseeable future? Or, as with us, is everything that touches on your personal life in the dark?

XIV. *from* ARNOLD HAASE

Berlin, April 5, 1933

I haven't had a chance until today to thank you for your telephone call on Sunday. I was delighted to be able to talk to you, and I can send you the following reassuring report:

The arrest of Dr. Michel and Dr. Wolff was carried out with the greatest propriety;[42] especially the behavior of the auxiliary police was impeccable, extremely polite and helpful; conduct in this and every case has been exemplary. This observation seems to me of particular value because I do not want a wrong impression being bandied about abroad. Everything has to be done to portray the situation in Germany accurately and dispel completely the horror stories that are propagated abroad and that have no doubt done Germany great harm. It's gratifying to see that Italy has been particularly reasonable in this respect; as our relations with Italy seem, indeed, in the best of order. You will doubtless have read in the German press what the intentions of the government are regarding the *Gleichschaltung* of the economic associations. It is altogether understandable that the government— or the appropriate officials—intervene in the work of the economic associations, that is, mainly insofar as questions of economic policy are involved. You will know from the papers about the situation of the National Industrial Association *(Reichsverband der Industrie)*, and it is altogether comprehensible and welcome as well that a close tie is being created between the competent governmental agencies and the key organizations in German industry.

New directors have taken over the Association of the Radio Industry,[43] and they will keep these offices from now on. For reasons of space, after amiable negotiations with the new directors, it was decided that I, along with the administration of the other associations, will move to the lower floor

---

[42] Dr. Michel and Dr. Wolff were directors of an agency for cartel administration in which Haase worked. Michel and Wolff were Jews; both were soon released but forced to give up their positions. Such enterprises were *gleichgeschaltet*, that is pro-Nazis were placed in leading positions.

[43] The Association of the Radio Industry (Funk-Industrie) was one of the associations that had been administered in Haase's office and was now removed from it. Another association, administered in this office, was the later-mentioned button industry.

and carry on my work there. All of us will, of course, do our best to carry out the tasks entrusted to us for the well-being of our industries, and so to create the foundation necessary for the revival of our sorely crippled industry.

I have particularly close ties to German industries that produce buttons and have, together with the concerned German agencies, managed to arrange negotiations with key Italian organizations of this industry. The meetings will probably take place in Milan in the first half of May. They will be private business talks similar to many that took place during the past year between representatives of German and French industry. We will work very hard to make clear to the Italians that the present flooding of the German market with cheap Italian goods is intolerable for us Germans, and we hope to be able to satisfy the interests of both industries either by arranging quotas or by some other friendly and economically rational agreement. I am not yet sure whether I will be able to participate in these negotiations. If I do, I would be most pleased if we could meet in Milan on this occasion, assuming you are still in Florence. . . .

I have been working too hard, and I'm a bit nervous and tired, so I'm very much looking forward to Easter when I'll go either to Buckow or Ferch for a few days' rest.[44] You will understand, my friend, why our plans for some Easter walks in Rome have fallen through, and I hope very much that it will soon be possible, after what will soon be two years, to have a break of a couple of weeks.

XV. *from* EDITH MENDELSSOHN BARTHOLDY

Leipzig, April 14, 1933

Thanks so much for your letter, which came to me opened but was still a great source of pleasure to me, for the most

---

[44] Villages on the lakes near Berlin.

important thing in our lives now is to have frequent good news from those close to us. There is not much cheerful news to look forward to, especially nothing to write about and neither time nor energy for such things. So it's all the more important to have at least short news as often as possible for you, Mämi, my brothers, and a few others.

I send you my warmest wishes for Easter and hope they find you in the best of spirits. I'm so pleased that you could be present for the opening of the Holy Year and could see the Pope. I hope you had a good place and have come away with pleasant memories. I wish life would open up for me again so that I could imagine myself in St. Peter's. If you read the *Deutsche Allgemeine Zeitung* regularly, you will have the best information about recent events here. The other papers contain little. Haase and Theodor have no doubt told you a great deal, but no descriptions can fully convey the impressions a historian really needs to have. I'm living a very quiet and retired life, seeing only the people who come to me in the gallery and sometimes a few other people who have the courage to be one's friend. There aren't many. A life like grandmother's goes on relatively unchanged, of course, but one who has always been in the thick of public life is completely torn out of its accustomed ways. Your disadvantage of missing out on these experiences is balanced by *not* having certain experiences. . . . It is not particularly edifying to see hysteria, cowardice, fear, and self-importance spreading into the most insignificant women's clubs . . . I have given up all my honorary offices. The Nazis tried to make trouble for me on the boycott day; however, their action was directed at the financial backer of the gallery rather than at me, and bothered me less than it bothered the large group of workmen who almost all are on the extreme Right politically. . . . So this attack hurt their own forces. However, now the financier has lost his enthusiasm and I'm supposed to liquidate. I'm trying to persuade him otherwise, but I doubt I'll succeed. Even the ministry agrees with me that an enterprise of this sort should not be allowed to go by the boards. But whether they're willing to maintain it with its present female manager is another question. The attempt will be made to create a livelihood for the widow of a cavalry captain who was killed in the war. . . . Will they succeed? I can't quite believe they will.

Things are very bad financially. At the moment I'm working entirely without pay to demonstrate that the business can turn a profit, and that is of course very hard, particularly because I don't know whether this work without pay will pay off in the end. . . . But even if I have to give up this little apartment and send Olga away,[45] I won't throw in the towel completely.

XVI. *from* THEODOR E. MOMMSEN

Bad Elinsberg, April 15, 1933

I'm on a short Easter holiday that I'm spending with my aunt Heidi in the Iser Mountains. After all these unsettling days, I'm enjoying the rest very much, and I'm trying now to take stock of what is going on beyond and behind all the day-by-day events that constantly overwhelm one.

It often happened in these last weeks that you broke down altogether, didn't know what to say, and knew only that you rejected all this in the depths of your being. I don't need to name the specific events. You know what they are, and you will know what my position on them was. There are things about which you know that you can't make any compromise. That is particularly true for the question of anti-Semitism, which has assumed such a massive role in recent events. Perhaps it was good—it was certainly necessary—that it came fully and clearly to light, particularly for those who were

[45] Her maid.

basically anti-Semitic but made the famous exception.[46] They
are now learning from experiences in their circle of friends
and relatives that no evasiveness, no wishy-washy compromise is possible. *Hic Rhodus, hic salta!* We were no doubt free
of this failing, but we too were perhaps all too ready to deny
the existence of a Jewish question. But that is a wide field
that will be the subject of many a future discussion for us.
For the time being, a massive process of transformation is
going on, one that we have to watch happening in a fright-
eningly large number of cases without being able to say or do
anything about it. I ate with A. a few days ago. He wants to
leave. He sees Zionism as the only possible path he can take
for his and his children's future. I can understand that decision, particularly in someone with the character he has. There
will be many of the very best who will choose this route. And
there is nothing anyone like us can say about it. I can't assess
either the internal or external possibilities. But what I can't
accept—and I said this to A.—is that this is the only path a
decent human being can take. You know my friend L. E. By
descent he is a pure Jew, and the family has been rooted in
German culture only a short time. But for all that, he is one
of the "best Germans" I know, almost nationalistic in his
affirmation of everything German and in his radical rejection
of all the visions of an international pan-European culture.
He has never been a Zionist, not even in his youth; he has
always rejected that possibility for himself and can't accept it
even now. He is a profoundly moral person and believes as
unconditionally as perhaps only a Jew can believe in the validity
of the moral laws to which all actions, even and especially
those of the state, should be subject. In the face of everything
that has happened he is broken, yet he still can't turn his
back on this country that casts him out as a pariah. In his
case, A.'s category of what any "decent" person must do sim-

[46] He alludes to the frequently heard remark "Oh, I am not anti-Semitic; X, who
is a Jew, is a friend of mine."

ply doesn't apply; I think a lot about this case because I am sure it is not an isolated case and because it will surely be significant for all of us in the future. But even in the face of these personal experiences we have to realize and keep in mind that the Jewish problem represents only one facet of the present development, though it is one that is of the greatest concern to us. We have to deal not only with the fiction of a racially purified Germany but with a governmental, economic, social, and intellectual reconstruction of the country, or at least that is supposedly what this is all about. The governmental reorganization is the starting point. It seems to me that the first step, the appointment of the *Reichsstatthalter,* still leaves every possibility open. If more is not done, then in a few years the *Reichsstatthalter* in Bavaria will represent Bavarian interests just as the Wittelsbachs, Eisner, Kahr, and Held once did.[47] The assertion of the federal government's authority will remain, as it has been up to now, a question of power, with, however, the crucial difference that the law now is much more clearly on the side of the federal government. But beyond this merely mechanical and formally undoubtedly clever and ingenious *Gleichschaltung,* which is only the consequence of dictatorship—for it is the nature of every dictatorship to have only *one* decision-making center—further organizational changes will be called for. That means, in my view, that those sources of particular resistance that after the end of princely rulers and the change in the role of the parliaments still exist, namely, the bureaucracies of the various states, will have to be eliminated by transferring the administration of police, law, and finances to the central government. In that case, we would have advanced a decisive step by this revolution, and, for our part, would have to acknowledge this. Certainly we can't make simply a plus and

[47] Eisner, Kahr, and Held were Bavarian prime ministers after 1918, and opposed interference by the federal government in Bavarian affairs. The Wittelsbachs were the dynasty that had ruled in Bavaria until 1918.

minus calculation. There are things that are and remain morally inexcusable but, on the other hand, must be recognized as historical facts; that is, as Hegel would say, the law of the "cunning of reason." We have still other problems that are in urgent need of solutions; and that fact seemed to me, as you know, to contain a strong psychological argument for the coming of a revolution; for only a temporary suspension of the legal order could and can advance these issues. Will it come to that? Everything is very, very unclear and gloomy. We can only hope, and we *must* hope. Otherwise, where should we be driven to? My reflections will perhaps strike you as strangely philosophical. But I'm trying to understand, but I can't take a position of rigid opposition (for the most varied of reasons, one among them being that we do, after all, have something like the whole of our lives before us). But to understand, I need philosophy, no matter how close to sophistry this may seem to be. One thing I firmly believe: total absurdities cannot exist. In other words, what is going on now either has or will acquire meaning, or . . . ?

But let me touch on a few concrete issues exclusive of foreign-policy matters, of which you will have a better grasp than I. I will mention, however, that there is general dismay over the recent debates in the English lower house.[48] Within Germany, the internal *Gleichschaltung* continues, with the Supreme Court, the Catholic church, and industry proving to be about the only centers of some resistance or at least of some reserve. Industry is obviously already preparing to accept exclusive National Socialist rule and write off the DNVP.[49] This prognosis is probably correct, as is the consideration that the only struggle likely to succeed must be carried out on the ground and within the organization by the dominant

[48] On Germany. Sir Austen Chamberlain said in this debate that revision of the Treaty of Versailles could no longer be considered.
[49] Deutsch-Nationale-Volks-Partei, the chief right-wing party before the Nazis took over leadership of the right.

trend, within which all opposing views will soon be "unified." What will this synthesis look like? The coming legis-
lation on the unions will give a first answer. Perhaps our new
national holiday has already provided a hint too?[50] What are
people in Italy saying about this? It is quite all right with
me. What will be of decisive importance is whether our rulers will be able to carry through their policy against our East
Elbian Junkers,[51] who have lost all their followers for the first
time—that was not the case in 1919. This too holds great
possibilities.

But it's impossible to write about all these things. One
has to talk about them. And I hope we'll be able to do just
that soon. On the twenty fourth I'll have my crucial meeting
with Kehr,[52] whom I'm going to ask to assign to me the
collection of all the materials pertaining to German-Italian
relations in the fourteenth century, a project that will certainly take more than a year and one that I find most attractive under the present circumstances. I'm anxious to see how
he'll react, and then when and if I can go. I'm still hoping
very much for a week or two in Rome as a starter. Perhaps
we'll see each other there. If not, we'll surely have several
weeks of work together in the Archivio di Stato in Florence.

XVII. *from* ERICH WRESCHNER

Berlin, April 28, 1933

I was very pleased about your prompt response. I have to
tell you that your letter was open when it arrived here. I was
unable to determine the reason: were you too sparing with

---

[50] The first day of May, formerly purely a workers' holiday, had been declared a
national holiday.
[51] He wonders whether the Nazis will be able to eliminate the influence of agrarian-
conservative circles, which had been strong under Hindenburg.
[52] Head of the Monumenta Germaniae Historica, where Mommsen worked as assistant.

your spit, or was the properly sealed envelope opened and then not resealed?

Your friend M. received me most cordially when I visited him and spoke with me about current problems. He also conveyed to me your concern about Lothar and your willingness to help Lothar out if things get serious for him.[53] I have appraised Lothar of your offer in a form that seemed appropriate to me. I'm sure I hardly need stress how extremely grateful he is to you. Just the feeling of not being all alone but of being able to count on friendly support gives one, in these days, a certain strength and confidence. I assume that Lothar has written to you directly in the meantime.

My view of your travel plans is precisely that of the correspondents whom you mentioned in your letter. You must include in your deliberations what your possibilities are for returning to Italy if you should come here. I don't really know whether you will be able to leave Germany again at your pleasure, whether you will need an exit visa, whether you can get one without difficulty, or whether the Italians could put any obstacles in the way of your reentry to Italy. I fully understand that the realization of your travel plans has a particular emotional and intellectual value for the people you want to see and talk with just now. On the other hand, you should take into account that the practical advantages of your appearing in Berlin should not be overestimated. The German papers correctly point out that we are still in the midst of the national revolution. This fact prevents us from reaching personal decisions of major importance. Until we are able to survey future developments with some certainty, it is, in my opinion, not possible to advise anyone to take decisive steps. My friends here and my colleagues who are in official positions take the view that one should wait for the time being. I think they are right. Therefore, it makes little

[53] Lothar's friends knew that his sudden dismissal from the judicial administration because he was a Jew placed him in a precarious financial situation.

practical sense for you to, as you put it, turn up here in the next few weeks. There are people who think too that it is more reasonable to stay where one is *extra muros,* ready to be available there if the need should arise. Well, you know the arguments for and against, and the final decision has to be yours alone.

I can fully understand your feelings. But I'm afraid even here you will not lie down with the pleasant feeling of having solid ground under your feet (I'm discovering too late that this image is poorly chosen, because one never sets one's feet on the ground if one is lying down). Everyone who is directly or indirectly affected—and there are many of them—is up in the air.

With that, I'll close my none too illuminating remarks for today.

XVIII. *from* MY SISTER

London, May 4, 1933

. . . Everyone coming from Germany speaks at length about the change in people's mood and appearance and about the widespread optimism. When I make a genuine effort to believe in the true unity of all the people and in the new feelings of community and not regard them as the products of terror and power, and when I consider as quite reasonable some of the things that have been done, for example, the constitutional reform (I would, however, have preferred South German hegemony), the year of labor service (of which you probably disapprove), the statements about the importance of the elementary school and the selective principle, the theories about labor (although I wonder what will be made of all these things in reality)[54]—despite these positive impressions, all I have to

[54] These are references to decrees of the federal government made during the preceding week. These decrees were against the overcrowding of schools and universities, which implied the institution of a *numerus clausus,* and for the institution of

do is open the newspaper and read the kind of sentences that appear in Ley's proclamation:[55] "The sly fox isn't fooling us; we prefer to finish him off with one final shot in the head. . . . Let the Leiparts pretend as much submission to Hitler as they will," the bombast, brutality, and tastelessness are without equal. Or "We regard it as our task to free our people from the inferiority complexes that were artificially instilled in them because they corresponded to the inferiority of the political parties." When I read this kind of thing, I can't understand how thinking people can even listen to these totally illogical, vapid, and false statements, and the conclusions they lead up to are downright dangerous. And what is happening at the universities is simply beyond description.[56] One thing that becomes very clear is that the Aryan race is not the one that has produced great people.

XIX. *from* LOTHAR PREUSS

Breslau, May 9, 1933

. . . You will be able to imagine what my psychic state is without my having to go into detail about it. That I am not completely abandoned in this situation helps me keep my courage up.

As you have probably heard from Mr. Mommsen, I have

a labor service, first on a voluntary basis. Some of these measures were carried out only in later months.

[55] On May 2 the houses and newspaper offices of the free trade unions (Socialist) were occupied by the SA and the auxiliary police. The orders had been given by Robert Ley, the leader of the National Socialist Labor Front, who then proclaimed the formation of a unified labor organization under National Socialist control. The quotations in this letter come from this proclamation. Leipart (the "sly fox") had been the leader of the free trade unions and had tried to come to some agreement with the National Socialists.

[56] The dismissals of university professors because of their political attitude or their race had begun in April and continued throughout the year. Among those dismissed in April were widely known scholars like Moritz Julius Bonn, Emil Lederer, Hans Kelsen, Egon Schmalenbach, Max Horkheimer, Karl Mannheim, Paul Tillich, Max Born, and Richard Courant.

moved to Breslau where I am working as an apprentice for my cousin Lutz Eisner. My cousin runs an agency for fabrics and similar materials. He gives me room and board and a little pocket money, and so I contrive to make a living. As you can well imagine, my present work isn't very agreeable for me. For one thing, I'm a complete tyro in this field, and every beginning shop girl knows what she's doing better than I do. You must try to forget the past entirely so that you learn to bear the difference from the past. Didn't we once write an essay called "The Art of Forgetting"? Then too the human element is so different. Politeness and good manners aren't particularly valued here. The worst of it, though, is the feeling that from no fault of my own I've been forced out of my profession to which over the years I had developed a deep attachment, and in which I no longer have the right to take part. And even if you hang on to a little hope, your reason tells you that such hope has no prospect. And yet for all that, I have to be thankful to have found this opportunity to earn my keep. But unfortunately even this new existence is not unthreatened.

I hope you will send word of yourself to me here so that we don't lose touch with each other completely. I don't have much else to report about my life. Erich gets the *Juristische Wochenschrift*[57] and sends it on to me so that we don't get entirely out of practice. And I read a little, Roth's *Radetzky-marsch* at the moment. A very well-written book. But I'm making my way through it very slowly because I don't have much free time.

Compared with Berlin, life in Breslau is, of course, incredibly provincial. That too is hard to bear. . . .

I'm hoping to hear from you soon.

[57] The leading German legal periodical.

XX. *from* KLAUS DOHRN

Rome, May 30, 1933

Many thanks for your card. Unfortunately, we are not trained graphologists and so could not decipher whether you will be in Florence for another week or a month. Inquiries to Holldack suggest, however, that it will be a month and that you will therefore still receive this letter on the Arno. It was a great pity that we didn't get a chance to see each other again, particularly if you are really determined to risk a journey among the aborigines of wildest central Europe, for which I must say you earn my unbounded admiration. . . .

How will I manage here in Rome if I can't talk politics and eat oysters in the Valle[58] with you every day? From the whole "political circle of Rome" only Holldack and I remain.[59] At any rate, we hope that you will soon rejoin us whenever the desire for more civilized regions seizes you again.

. . . *The problems* that the political upheaval has created for people like us—the nerve, the self-confidence, the optimism that it has cost us—we will probably be able to assess in its whole length, width, and depth only at some later date. And only now can we begin to assess slowly how deep Germany's fall is not only in political but also in cultural respects. Particularly on this account I can hardly wait for your eyewitness reports "from the German bush with flashbulb and flintlock."

Sooner or later we will all be faced, in one form or another, with the crucial question: What next? Our political activity clearly can't consist in mere fruitless negation or in complaining every night over glasses of Castelli wines. Thinking we

[58] A restaurant in Rome that, if I remember correctly, opened only late at night.
[59] Dohrn lived in a third- or fourth-floor apartment on the Piazza Navona. It had a large balcony overlooking the piazza, and Dohrn, Holldack, and I used to sit on this balcony at night, frequently until sunrise, discussing politics. Holldack's reports to his newspaper frequently began: "It is said in Roman political circles"; he then reported what we had discussed on the balcony.

can afford ourselves the luxury of political disinterest strikes me as an illusion, and "accommodation" [*Gleichschaltung*], for me anyhow, is completely and absolutely impossible. Sooner or later these three considerations will have to give rise to an initiative for fruitful, active opposition from abroad, to an action of exiles, with total commitment of our energies. It would be nice if we could meet again in such a context, and I think our shared days in Rome may well have created the human basis for this work.

For my part, I can hardly imagine such work taking place anywhere but in Austria, and being pro-Austria. I do not think Vienna will go along with the Nazis. Austria's determination to provide a platform for the "exiles," and not just the Catholics, with the purpose of reconstructing Germany seems firm to me.

I would be interested to hear what you have to say to all this, and whether you would be willing to take part in it if the possibility for it presented itself.—Or has the spectacle of the bizarre goings-on in Germany so paralyzed us all that we can do no more than be horrified onlookers? I would find that the equivalent of intellectual suicide.

XXI. *from* HEINZ TRÜTZSCHLER VON FALKENSTEIN

Geneva, June 13, 1933

I've just received your card from Florence, and I'm answering you immediately to say that I'm still in Geneva and that you should send me your letter right away. I'm so pleased to hear from you. I had thought you would still be in Italy, but I wasn't sure. My wife is leaving early next week to spend two weeks in Berlin, and I asked her to find out your address from Holborn or someone else. I have a great need to refortify our relationship, which has suffered, externally anyhow, because of my failings as a correspondent. The need to stick together is particularly great in these shaky, uncertain times, and if there is one thing that makes them easier to cope with, it is intellectual companionship. Letters from friends who are still in Germany are quite meaningless. So I'm doubly happy to hear from you, and I only wish we could meet somewhere in the coming months. How about a weekend somewhere on the northern Italian lakes? That must be just about halfway between Geneva and Florence.

All I want to say very briefly today is that things are going famously for me, apart from the great inner distress I feel. We are enjoying our agreeable and—thanks to a League of Nations contract that will run for almost another four years— secure life in Geneva more than ever. I'm still in the information section and have a great deal to do. Wertheimer[60] has been transferred to the financial section, and as a consequence I am for the time being alone—and will remain so at least until September. So for all practical purposes I'm my own boss. I'm very much enjoying the responsibility that comes with that, and because the German disarmament delegation is the old one and extremely moderate and reasonable, everything is going superbly. I hope that will continue to be so for as long as possible. Otherwise our political situation is very difficult and serious, perhaps more so than it may appear from Italy. But it's best not to think too much about the future. All the people who are coming from Germany are looking ahead to the winter with nothing but worry and despair.

XXII. *from* MY SISTER

London {no date}

Well, *alea jacta est*. I've taken the position at Bedford College. Perhaps it was stupid of me. I'm feeling very uncertain

---

[60] Another German official on the staff of the League of Nations.

about it, as I always do after any decision, but Miss Freund thinks I made the right choice. I'll tell you the disadvantages first: (1) I get no salary but I do get free room and board. That makes me financially not much worse off than I was before. I find {living in} the college hard to take, of course, but I console myself with the thought that it will be interesting to see a place like this from within, and then I'm "staff," so I'm not tied down by the regulations. (2) This is a position that up to now has been filled by a student who was just about to take her exams. In other words, I'm "above" the job, but we have clarified this point, and I will be treated, in keeping with my age and degrees, as a faculty member, and I get on very well with the professor who has already agreed to hand over to me some of her more advanced classes (I'll teach only eight hours per week). The third German teacher will be a very young lecturer—so the work may be fun, and I think I'll be able to make it a real position.

The advantages are that I can attend all courses for free, including a very expensive phonetics course I very much wanted to take this year, and that I may be able to acquire an English degree, which could be advantageous in the future. Then too I'll be in contact with a lot of interesting people.

If I weigh all the pluses and minuses, this is of course not a fully satisfying job, and once again I won't be completely on my own in it. That would have been the nice thing about the school job,[61] where I would have built up the German program. But at the moment I have nothing against enjoying life a bit more and taking things easier. I can use a little more ease, and this will be an interesting experiment. The school job would have been a more solid proposition, but whether I would get it was uncertain. I had still another very vague offer—an American millionairess who wanted to start a school, but that was totally vague and in the country. It would have

[61] My sister had received some "feelers" for a teaching position at a school in London.

been nothing but work. I don't know the lady at all. Acquaintances of mine put me in touch with her. At any rate, I'll leave it hanging for now. It is a tempting offer. Financially I'm all set until Christmas because I have a radio contract, five pounds a month.[62] All in all, I guess I should count myself lucky because I don't think Germany is an option for me now, judging from what everyone tells me. And to be in London again is good luck. Only I had pictured myself living in a beautiful flat. Dr. Massey,[63] whom I've been telling about you, suggested, as a consolation, a place in a nearby boarding house. . . . And now, in all seriousness, why don't you give England a try? Without connections there's not much one can do, but with them you may be able to get something, and a year of research work or work for a magazine wouldn't be such a bad thing. I have the impression something could be done, but you've got to strike while people are still worked up about what is happening in Germany. You'd like the political climate here. . . .

[62] My sister gave German lessons on the London radio.
[63] Isabel Massey, Reader in German at Bedford College, friend and translator of Gaetano Salvemini, was a friend of my sister. Since my sister's acceptance of the Bedford offer made it impossible for us to take an apartment in London together, as she had planned, Dr. Massey had suggested a boarding house in London near Bedford College for me if I should come to London.

Chapter VI

London
in Peace,
London
in War

I

THE LAST significant political event that took place while I was still in Germany was the Nazi government's withdrawal from the Disarmament Conference and from the League of Nations on October 14, 1933. Shortly afterward I left Berlin and traveled to London. Of my voyage to England, and even of my arrival in London—the railroad station, my first encounter with a London taxi, and my first impression of London streets—I have no memory. The departure from Germany loomed so overwhelmingly in my mind that I had not much sense of what was going on around me.

During my first days in London I had been invited to stay with the mother of an aunt of mine. She was German-born but had married an Englishman and become a British subject; her household, however, was still conducted in a very

German manner. When I settled down in a guest room I felt relieved that I had not been thrown into a completely foreign world. Hyde Park was within a few minutes' walk of the house. On one of my first days in London, I took a walk in the park with my friend Holborn; like me, he was in search of a position outside Nazi Germany. It was a gray, wet day, and everything was enveloped in fog. Of course we talked mainly about politics, and this too was not a joyful subject. It was a grim walk, and it became embedded in my mind because its cheerless gray remained the dominant tone of the two years I spent in London. It was unfortunate that I arrived in London for the first time in the autumn after having spent a good part of the spring and summer in Italy. The grayness of London's rain and fog seemed to reduce me to a lower level of awareness and reaction. I shall never forget the overpowering impression of color and vitality I felt when on my first visit to London's National Gallery I saw its great Veroneses and felt closer again to the land I loved.

I am quite aware that there were psychological reasons why I was unappreciative, critical, and negative during my two years in London. Unhappiness about leaving Germany on the one hand, the need to find a way to exist and work in an alien country on the other, were always at the back of my reactions to what I saw and experienced there. My description of peacetime London is subjective and biased, but I cannot omit these years from the story of my life. Living in a big city without the security of being surrounded by family and friends and having to face reality without illusions provided a necessary education—a precondition for building a new life in a new country.

When I recall my stay in London the impression I have is that I spent most of my time in the underground. London not only had more inhabitants than Berlin, but because most of its residents lived in small private houses London extended over a much wider area. The underground was the chief means of getting from one part of town to the other. Most of the time there I lived in rented rooms, mainly in Hampstead, which was too far from the center to walk; the underground was the quickest way of getting into town. This meant riding down into what seemed the bottom of the earth on elevators or moving stairs, their walls embellished by colorful advertisements that showed beautiful ladies in swimming suits or men in seductively warm sweaters, and my favorite: in a row of pale and hungry soldiers, one, rosy-cheeked and self-satisfied, stands out; an army officer, red in the face and near a stroke, shouts in the caption, "Who has been at my Enos?" Changing trains underground, a frequent necessity, meant walking through dirty tunnels and up and down filthy staircases. Even after reaching the desired platform the ordeal was not over because two or three overcrowded trains might pass before you could squeeze into a compartment.

The underground became a life-controlling monster in still other ways. The last trains ran between 11:00 P.M. and midnight. I had always been a night owl, a person who at parties "woke up" very late but then enjoyed the give and take of a lively, sometimes heated discussion, or who after a concert or the theater needed to ruminate in a bar or restaurant about what he had heard or seen. The rush to get the last underground at eleven seemed to me an impoverishment of life, or at least a diminution of pleasure.

A further, and perhaps more serious, worry was the shocking expensiveness of London, where my financial reserves shrank quickly. I had often heard that life in London was costly, but, perhaps on the basis of my Italian experiences, I must have formed some primitive ideas about the expense of life outside Germany. During the preceding eight years I had been relatively free from this kind of anxiety. After the death of my mother in 1923, I had inherited a small capital. Although its income did not fully cover the expenses of the following years of study and research, I had filled the gap by selling some shares. I did this without much hesitation because I was quite confident that I would be able to get a salaried position, and because I could expect to inherit further a not inconsiderable sum of money. The economic crisis, together with the restrictions the Nazi government placed on the transfer of money to foreign countries, worsened my financial situation. You could take your money out of Germany only if you gave a good part of your capital to the Nazi government. Whether it was possible to circumvent these restrictions by illegal means I am not sure; I did not consider such a possibility, perhaps because it would have been dangerous for relations who remained in Germany, but mainly because I felt a strong personal urge to make the break with Nazi Germany as quickly and as cleanly as possible. In London I soon came to realize that my financial reserves would not last long.

The obvious necessity to be very cautious about my expenses was not without influence on the picture I developed of English society. That rich people can do things less fortunate people cannot afford to do is no great discovery, and luxurious hotels and restaurants were not the kinds of places I had ever frequented. I was struck in London, however, by the strict separation of those places frequented by high society from those open to all others, by the sharp distinction of an upper group from all the other, by no means impoverished, groups of society. It seemed to me not only that—to use a well-worn formula—the world of the masses was divided from the world of the classes, but also that the world of the classes was strictly divided. English snobbism is a well-known phenomenon, but the extent to which it existed and manifested itself surprised me. While staying in a rented room in a boarding house I soon discovered that it was a matter of pure chance whether telephone messages would be noted down and reported. However, when a lord—the only lord with whom I was acquainted, a young man whom I had met through relations in Berlin—telephoned, I had hardly entered the house before the maid or the lady of the house appeared to tell me of his call. The frankness with which people categorized others—acquaintances or even friends—as "middle class," "upper middle class," or "lower middle class" astonished me.

I—and I suppose many people who come from the Continent to England—find it tempting to speculate how liberal and democratic values can coexist with a society of hierarchically organized classes. My theory was that consensus about the rightness of the entire structure so permeated British life that each of its component parts was believed to have a necessary and justifiable place. Perhaps the experience of living on an island separated from other nations kept alive among the British traces of the romantic notion that society formed an organic whole. A positive attitude toward the existence of a structured society made the individual inclined to accept, or at least adjust to, the standards and the behavior of his or her class. My sister had succeeded beautifully in fitting herself into English life. I sometimes asked her about the appropriate response to a request, or an invitation, or about other aspects of everyday behavior. She usually replied: "*We* do it that way," to which I responded, annoying her: "What does 'we' mean, who is 'we'?"

Of course, I developed only gradually a coherent picture of England—distorted as it might have been. What was clear to me from the outset was that I felt rather distant toward England; I was aware therefore that I had to make a strenuous effort to understand the world around me, and to overcome my ambiguous feelings toward a life that seemed admirable and unacceptable at the same time. I knew that in order to develop a better understanding of England I had to improve my knowledge of the English language. As children my sister and I had had briefly an English governess; we chattered happily in English, and I can still quote English children's songs I learned at that time. Whereas my sister went on to study English at the university, I did nothing to maintain or improve my knowledge of the language, although strangely enough I have always been able to read English scholarly books that I needed for my work. My spoken English was, however, in a deplorable state.

During my first months in London I took English lessons daily. I tried to restrict all my reading to books in English, and my discovery of English literature was one of the happy aspects of my life during these years. In my explorations in this field I had remarkably good guidance: my sister had arranged for my renting a room in the house of the poet Wilfred Gibson. The Gibsons, who lived with their three teen-aged children, were lovely people. I cannot deny that the meals I took with them (breakfast and, twice a week, supper) were rather puritan for my taste. I particularly detested the stewed prunes at breakfast, which I was told were good for the digestion. Topics of conversation were not always easy to find. However, the Gibsons were kind enough to correct my English and to insist on making me better acquainted with English literature. In the afternoons Mrs. Gibson frequently read to me and the children. Once she chose D. H. Lawrence's *The Prussian Officer*—evidently without ever having read the story before—because she hoped the subject would be of interest to me. When in the course of reading aloud she discovered that the story was about homosexuality she suddenly broke off, remarking she had something important to do. I suspected that the sudden interruption of the reading had some deeper reasons, and I finished the story myself. But for days the children wondered why they never heard how the story ended. Mr. Gibson acted as my guide to British literature—and I shall always be thankful to him. Before coming to England my knowledge of the literature was more or less restricted to Dickens, Scott, and Galsworthy. Mr. Gibson's first advice to me was to read *Wuthering Heights,* which he considered as somewhat in the style of the German romantics. Indeed, I was impressed, and from there we went on to all the Brontës, to Jane Austen, and George Meredith; I soon discovered *Tristram Shandy* and *Vanity Fair,* which have been favorite books of mine ever since.

Without the Gibsons I might not have found my way quickly into the older English literature, but modern literature, which meant Bloomsbury at that time, came up frequently in conversations. I was enthusiastic when *Mrs. Dalloway* and *To the Lighthouse* first came into my hands, and I waited with excitement for every new book by Virginia Woolf. I was moved by Rosamond Lehman's *Dusty Answer.* In recent years I haven't looked at any of these novels because I fear that I may have overestimated them; I don't want to have to admit to myself that these books, which I remember as emotional and intellectual experiences, are not the great works of art I believed them to be.

The discovery of English literature helped me develop some understanding for what at the beginning had seemed to me a very strange style of life. But politics was the focal point of my effort to understand what was going on in England, as was natural for someone who had grown up in the turbulent years of the First World War and the Weimar Republic. A close tie between present and past seemed to me the most distinguishing feature of English political life. That was certainly my impression as I stood in the street watching the procession of the Lord Mayor's Show, the opening of Parliament, or a memorial service in St. Paul's Cathedral. It struck me that in England historical tradition is created not only by recalling the memory of great leaders and celebrating great events, but also by the survival and continuation of the forms observed in the conduct of public business—whether in Parliament, in the law courts, or in the universities. One is continuously aware of living in a society of a very individual character, distinct from all others. Being a member of this society gives a person a special character and unique value.

I was still in London when King George V died in January

1936. In a cold rain, people stood for many hours along the Thames in a long queue that hardly moved at all. Finally the queue crossed the bridge, entered the Parliament building, and silently moved through the hall where the king was lying in state. As at all such occasions, curiosity and sensationalism certainly played a part—I cannot deny that my own participation in this long ordeal was to a large extent due to curiosity—but for many, taking part in this demonstration was an expression of their attachment and respect for this particular king. I felt very strongly, however, that most of those who moved slowly along in this long, silent line were not led by any particular sentiment, nor did they intend to demonstrate anything; the monarchy was for them an integral part of English life, and participation in the funeral of the king was the same as what you did when a death occurred in your family.

Of course I was particularly interested in the British reaction to the rise of the Nazis in Germany and in what they intended to do about it. I tried to explore the British political scene in a variety of ways. I spent Sunday mornings at Hyde Park Corner and listened to what the "men of the people" (strangely enough, I don't remember a woman speaking there) had to say. I went to Labour Party meetings in East London, and I stood on the street watching demonstrations against war and for disarmament. An amusing moment in this "study of English politics" came during a meeting of the Fabian Society, which was celebrating the fiftieth anniversary of its formation. One of the main speakers was George Bernard Shaw, who was sitting on the rostrum together with the society's founding fathers: Sidney Webb, who had become Lord Passfield, and Sidney Olivier, who was Lord Olivier. Shaw began his speech with "Ladies and gentlemen" and then, interrupting himself, said: "I see I must say 'My lords, ladies, and gentlemen.' " This speech changed my view of Shaw, whom I had known only as a writer of a number of witty but

also rather lighthearted plays; I became aware of the seriousness of the radical views behind his satire.

The most memorable of my political lessons was a visit to
the House of Commons. I had the good luck to be present at
the debate in which Stanley Baldwin made his famous state-
ment, which soon proved to be mere rhetoric: "Our frontier
is on the Rhine." The most impressive speaker in the debate
was Winston Churchill, who warned of the consequences of
German rearmament. Since I had heard that Churchill was
one of the most impressive speakers in the House of Commons, I was at first disappointed when he rose and began his
speech. He spoke slowly, almost haltingly; he seemed to be
searching for words; gradually, however, the tempo increased,
and he slowly moved from the back benches closer to the
table in the center. The sentences became longer and more
complicated, and the speech rose to a crescendo at the end.
When he sat down and the discussion returned to its normal
level, I felt let down—as from a high plateau to a low plain.
After that I heard Churchill speak several times; I always
listened with great admiration, but no impression was as strong
as the one I experienced when I heard him for the first time
while sitting in the gallery of the House of Commons.

If my study of the English political scene focused on
England's attitude toward the Nazi government, this was more
than the natural reaction of a refugee from Nazi Germany; it
had concrete practical reasons. My friend from our months in
Rome, Klaus Dohrn, had carried out the plan he had outlined to me in the spring of 1933. Under the aegis of his
uncle, Dietrich von Hildebrand, he was beginning to edit a
political weekly in Vienna opposing the Nazis. I wrote a few
articles for this periodical, and I reported regularly on the
English political situation. Discussing what the English might
do in the crisis brought about by the rise of the Nazis was
not a superfluous task, but of some practical importance. The
indignation that English public opinion—from Conservative

to Labour—expressed over the Nazi persecution of the Jews and over the Nazi suppression of freedom and democracy created the expectation in many that the English were willing and ready to take a decisive stand against the Nazis. In Austria, where Chancellor Dollfuss was holding out against the Nazis and conducting a policy that incensed Hitler, the question of whether and to what extent Austria could count on British support was crucial.

There was no easy answer, however. During my years in England—and actually beyond these years until 1939—British policy toward Germany presented an utterly confusing picture. Protests and actions such as the formation of the Stresa Front, which envisaged England's cooperation with France and Italy against German rearmament and aggressiveness, were followed by inaction, by visits of British ministers to Germany, and, in 1935, by the conclusion of an Anglo-German naval agreement. Furthermore, the emergence of a British Fascist movement was a disturbing phenomenon even if one could discount for the foreseeable future the influence of Mosley's Blackshirts. Britain's contradictory actions could not lead to great hopes for a resolute anti-Nazi policy. The Labour Party was the most pronounced anti-Nazi force in British politics, but it was permeated by a moralistic pacifism that indulged in illusions about international cooperation.

The conflict between Italy and Abyssinia showed these contradictions very clearly. I had some knowledge of Italian politics, and it seemed to me evident that two possibilities existed. The first was to allow Mussolini the conquest of Abyssinia, which for at least some time would ensure his cooperation against Nazi Germany; Mussolini was disquieted by German support of the Austrian Nazi movement and its possible consequence—the reunion of Austria and Germany. If England believed, however, that the maintenance of international law was its highest duty and the only way of avoiding military conflicts among the great powers, then Italian aggression had to be condemned and a policy of sanctions had to be pursued; in this case, England had to be prepared for an armed conflict with Italy. Although I was convinced and am still convinced that Mussolini would have given in had the second option been taken, at the time nobody could be sure. An energetic approach involved the risk of war. What seemed to me unquestionable, though, was that the policy Britain—the government with the support of Labour—carried out, that of opposing Mussolini's Abyssinian adventure only with protests and indecisive measures, was terribly wrong; it showed Mussolini that he could not rely on Britain when Germany turned to the absorption of Austria. As much as the leaders of the Labour Party detested the Nazi regime, fear of war and an illusory internationalism prevented many of them from approving measures which might lead to military conflict.

The Conservative policy—the policy of the government—was also based on misconceptions. The government undoubtedly disapproved of the Nazi regime, but the government could not or would not understand that what was happening inside Germany was of decisive importance for foreign policy. They saw no reason why Germany should not continue to play the role in the European balance of power that it had played before 1933: that of preventing French domination of Europe, and allowing Britain to be an arbiter in European affairs. The Conservatives did not see that the ruthless brutality the Nazis showed in their domestic policy permitted them quickly to build up a power apparatus that altered the entire European system of power.

Of course, British policy was less uniform than I have indicated. In the Liberal Party there were lively discussions about the extent to which pacifism could be pursued under the present circumstances. Among the Conservatives the group around Churchill had no illusions about the effects of the rise of Nazism. Moreover, there were tensions within the government,

with Sir John Simon and Anthony Eden as protagonists of
different approaches to the Nazi problem. It was an interesting, exciting experience to observe the evolution of British
responses to Nazi Germany, and to analyze the views of the
various public figures. Because I considered it necessary to
take a stand against the Nazis before they became militarily
powerful, I did not really expect the British to do what in
my opinion was required.

My views had been influenced to a certain extent by a conversation I had had shortly after my arrival in London. During an interview with a well-known English historian, our
talk turned to politics and I remarked that it was obvious
that Hitler's policy would create a situation in which war was
unavoidable; I added that Hitler was not a person to shy away
from war. I was strongly rebuffed, and told that my views
were clearly colored by my personal situation, with which he
had strong sympathy. However, my situation, he told me,
made me prejudiced and unable to evaluate correctly the
political scene. I was told I should refrain from discussing
such a subject. I am quite sure that the person who gave me
this advice had no sympathy for the Nazis or Fascism. In his
view, however, the Germans, like most non-English people,
had always had rather low standards of political behavior.
Although their victims deserved full sympathy, the Nazis
were not much worse than the Germans had always been.
This view expressed a kind of national arrogance that veiled
understanding of what was going on in Germany. I was not
the only one who had this kind of depressing experience. My
uncle, Albrecht Mendelssohn Bartholdy, was almost better
known in the United States and England than in Germany.
In 1933 he was quickly invited to come to England, and was
elected a fellow of Balliol College at Oxford. His Hamburg
Institute of Foreign Policy had cooperated closely with the
Chatham House in London, of which Arnold Toynbee was
director. In 1935 Toynbee visited Germany, where he had an

interview with Hitler, and when Toynbee returned to London Albrecht went to see him to hear about his impressions. I was curious to hear what Toynbee had reported to Albrecht, and we arranged to meet after his talk with Toynbee. So I waited on St. James' Square for my uncle. When he finally emerged from Chatham House, his first words were: "It is quite hopeless; they simply don't understand."

As I have said before, all this is something of a simplification. Certainly there were many people in England with wide political understanding, with whom you could have interesting discussions about politics. Still, I think that fundamentally my description of the English inability and unwillingness to understand what was happening in Germany is correct. There were, as historical investigations have shown, many reasons for the appeasement policy that developed through the 1930s to its fateful culmination in the Conference of Munich. I am convinced, however, that at bottom was the attitude that struck me repeatedly in my discussions in London: a combination of ignorance and arrogance.

The political climate I encountered during these years in London troubled me immensely; it was one of the factors that made it difficult for me to imagine that I could spend the rest of my life in England.

I was aware then—and am still more aware of it now, fifty years later—that my critical attitude toward England contained an element of sour grapes. My attitude would certainly have been more positive if I had had the feeling that an academic career was possible for me in England. Actually what the British did for the German refugees was admirable and deserves the deepest gratitude. Undoubtedly they were right in assuming that the United States was the country with the greatest possibilities for German academic refugees, that America could absorb them in greater numbers, and that because of the role foreign scholars had always played in America, they would have a wider sphere of action and influence there. England was to be viewed as a temporary stop rather than a place of final settlement. England did take a number of famous scholars—among them the classicist Eduard Fränkel, the physicist Max Born, the sociologist Karl Mannheim—as well as a few experts in special fields that were weak in England. Otherwise, the British concentrated on providing support for refugees until they could settle in America. However, such planning rested on insecure grounds. The increasingly brutal measures of the Nazi Party steadily added to the numbers of those forced to leave Germany, and the stream of academic refugees never seemed to end. At the same time, academic life in America was still suffering from the consequences of the depression; immigration visas could not easily be obtained, though in fact this was less difficult than rumor had it. Moreover, this was not yet the time of airplanes. America was still far away, and for those like myself who had never been on the other side of the ocean, the United States was an unknown quantity. Going there meant a much more decisive rupture from the world in which one had grown up and lived than crossing the channel between the European continent and the British Isles.

There was hardly a German academic refugee who did not spend the first months and years in England absorbed in the search for a job there. I was no exception, and after my arrival in England, I spent a good part of my time exploring such possibilities. How to behave when requesting a favor is something one learns only slowly in life, and I am afraid that my talents in this respect have never been great. I certainly was a bad petitioner in England. Moreover, I was aware—and I am sure others were too—that mine was not a particularly urgent case. Others who arrived with families and without any resources were in a more precarious situation. The chief reason, however, for my inability to establish successful contacts was the character of my work. I did not expect my concern with nineteenth-century German intellectual history, and particularly with the development of German historiography, to arouse great interest in England. But my other chief interest, the Italian Renaissance, and particularly Machiavelli and Guicciardini as leading figures in the political thinking of the time, seemed to me an "international" subject. This is certainly true now, but during the five decades since I lived in London the study of the Renaissance, particularly of the Italian Renaissance, has undergone an astonishing development in England, and still more in America. In both countries it has become a field of central importance in historical research since the Second World War, a position it had held in Germany and Italy since the last decades of the nineteenth century. I was surprised and somewhat shocked when I discovered that in England in the 1930s study of the Renaissance was left almost exclusively to art and literary historians. Machiavelli seemed a somewhat questionable subject; although it could not be denied that he stood at the beginning of modern political thought, he was not in the line of Grotius, Locke, or Adam Smith, which made human freedom a cornerstone of political life. The suspicion that had been dominant in the sixteenth and seventeenth centuries, that Machiavelli was really an advocate of the devil, lingered on.

The fact that my interests lay somewhat outside those of the English historical world strengthened in me the tendency to remain an outsider, following my own path. I sought refuge in the Reading Room of the British Museum, where I could have any book I wanted, and where I seemed to exist in a world of my own. I still remember the old lady, her face hidden behind a veil, who would arrive with a little pot of flowers which she placed on her desk, and the old gentleman who wore a sailor's cap and from whom you had to sit as far away as possible because he talked uninterruptedly, usually rather quietly, though every twenty or thirty minutes he raised his voice to a shriek. Nevertheless, it was an immense relief to spend a few hours every day in a place on which the events of the outside did not impinge and where, in studying the work of the humanists, I could sometimes imagine that I was still in my beloved Italy. When I felt I needed an interruption I walked a few steps into the hall where the Elgin Marbles stood, and they gave the wonderful assurance that the world in which the Nazis dominated was not the only world that existed.

However, the British Museum was not as removed from the contemporary world as these remarks might suggest. Opposite the British Museum, in Little Museum Street, was the bookshop of Hans Preiss. The owner had worked in a bookshop near the University of Berlin and was known, if only by sight, to many who had studied and taught there. He had come to England as soon as the Nazis had seized power, and opened his own bookshop. We always found there the latest political literature from the Continent as well as German literature. Although pamphlets and periodicals were scattered on bookcases and tables in what was a rather small room, there was always enough space to stand in a corner and flip through an article in some new publication, or get into conversation with others; Preiss' bookshop was a center for German intellectual refugees, and you could always be sure to get involved in a political discussion, frequently without knowing with whom. I believe Preiss initiated the arrangement of evening discussions in which an attempt was made to place the contemporary scene in perspective. Two of the speakers at these meetings were particularly impressive: Franz Borkenau, an expert on Communism in Spain, who was a remarkably unorthodox Marxist, and Franz Neumann, a political scientist and former German trade union lawyer. At the time, I exchanged only a few words with Neumann, with whom I would be closely associated in the Office of Strategic Services during the Second World War, when we would become good friends.

In order to understand the excitement of these discussions it should be remembered that until the death of Hindenburg in 1934 hopes continued to exist that the Nazi regime might be overthrown. Moreover, it should be recalled that conscription was reintroduced in Germany only in 1935, and that the Rhineland was reoccupied only in March 1936. Before these events had taken place a firm stand might have led to the fall of the Nazi regime. With the successful progress of Nazi foreign policy, however, the chances for a change in Germany were disappearing. I found, though, that as long as I lived near Germany and moved among people who, like me, had grown up there and been forced to leave, it was almost impossible not to remain obsessed with the Nazi problem, and to speculate endlessly on the future course of events. It was almost impossible to regain a sense of proportion and even freedom. Distance was necessary: I had to remove myself from the European scene as far as possible.

In 1936 the offer of a teaching job at a college in southern California came as a godsend, not only because it was a position that, at least temporarily, provided economic security and some chance of continuing my work in history, but also because it meant leaving Europe far behind. The immense relief I felt in getting away from Europe I find, in retrospect, astonishing. Travel between the United States and Europe was still a difficult enterprise that could not be frequently undertaken. The American West was still very far away and what was beyond the Rocky Mountains seemed to be on the other side of the globe; I knew not a single person in California, and had no clear idea about the job that awaited me. Yet in August 1936 as my ship was leaving Cobh, its last European port, I was sitting on my deck chair and realized with immense relief that this might be the last time I ever saw the coast of Europe.

II

WHEN I returned to Europe it was during the war. I was an American citizen and I had settled in the United States.

I now knew a good part of the country that had been *terra incognita* for me in 1936. After teaching for a year in California, on my trip back to the East, I got for the first time a feeling of what the United States were. Crossing the North American continent by car with an English friend of mine was an unforgettable experience. From Utah, with its serious, unsmiling Mormons and the heavy, still water of the Salt Lake, we drove on to a small village high in the mountains and quite remote from other settlements. A festival was going on in the village, and we told a young man who was helping us repair our car that he should go take part in the celebration. But he refused: "No, to be together with two people from Europe is much more exciting." As we drove through the mountains of Colorado there came a moment when suddenly the view opened on the great plain, which seemed to spread before us into the infinite like the Pacific Ocean we had left behind the week before. There followed the monotonous drive extending for days through the plain, on wide, straight highways that seemed to have no beginning and no end. An occasional church steeple or farmhouse were the only signs that people lived there. It was a very long, fascinating, and terrifying road from the lonely mountain villages of the West to the cities of the East, crowded with people from all parts of the earth.

The years between this trip (1937) and America's entry into the war were dominated by the debate between isolationism and interventionism. I was then an assistant to Edward Earle, professor at the Institute for Advanced Study in Princeton. Earle had arranged a seminar in which political scientists and historians discussed American attitudes toward the conduct of foreign affairs. An aim of these meetings was to demonstrate that, above and beyond ideology, the notion of national security ought to serve as the guiding criterion determining the course of foreign policy; this shifting of the debate on foreign policy from an ideological to a pragmatic level had its importance in these pre-war years, when consensus was needed about the course to be pursued.

During this period of Nazi expansion and aggression American foreign policy became a chief concern of mine. I was fascinated by the origins of the two contradictory ideological approaches to American foreign policy that were dominating the public debate. This interest was probably stimulated by the impressions I had received on my trip across the country. I had seen the reality that lay behind the wish to live apart from the temptations of the world, and behind the hope to build in America a new and better world. I had begun to understand the motives inspiring the settlement of the New World and the conditions that kept these attitudes alive. It also became clear that these attitudes had their roots in views and thoughts developed in the European past before the New World was settled. I became aware of the European experiences that lay behind the isolationism and Messianism of the American outlook on foreign affairs. I delivered some papers on this topic in Earle's seminar, published some articles, and finally gathered these studies into a book, *To the Farewell Address; Ideas of Early American Foreign Policy,* which was published, however, only twenty years later.

Whatever the value of these studies, they had great personal importance for me. In teaching European history in the United States I could not help wondering why the young people sitting before me should find the subject I taught them relevant to the world in which they were living. By studying the connections between the European and the American past, I felt reaffirmed in the significance of what I was doing. I might add that I never thought I knew anything about a country if I didn't know its history, whereas contributing to the understanding of a country's history gives one a feeling of being at home. When, during the war, I left the United States for Europe, I did not feel that I was going home. It was clear to me that after the war I would return to the United States.

III

ONCE the United States had entered the conflict, I was most anxious to take part in the war effort. After finally obtaining American citizenship, recommendations from Earle, Holborn, and other friends helped me to get a position in the Office of Strategic Services (OSS). I worked for a year in Washington in the Central European Section of the Research and Analysis Branch, analyzing and evaluating European developments on the basis of the reports we received. I was anxious to get nearer to the war and was very satisfied when in February 1944, I was sent to the London headquarters of the OSS. I sailed on the *Queen Elizabeth,* which was then being used as a troopship. The voyage was stormy, and after four days of traveling on a zigzag course to avoid being the target of submarines, we saw the northern coast of Ireland. We landed in Glasgow, and the welcome was more elaborate than the one I had received eleven years before on my first visit to British soil. Tea, coffee, and sandwiches served by uniformed young women were offered to us first in the Glasgow station and then in just about every station at which the train stopped on the long trip down to London. The final stop was at a depot outside London, where we boarded a bus that carried us through blacked-out streets to a rooming house in Kensington. Without looking around, I went to bed and fell asleep immediately. A real look at wartime London had to wait until the next morning.

Memory is an uncertain guide. In my recollection of wartime London the damage and destruction brought about by bombing attacks is not as prominent as perhaps it should be and probably was. These impressions paled somewhat compared with what I saw one year later in Germany. Yet the war, of course, dominates my memories of London in 1944–45. My office was on Brook Street, near Grosvenor Square, and during the first months of my stay I lived in a rented room on a street running off from Bayswater, north of Hyde Park. From the office to my boarding home was a walk of twenty minutes. I generally left the office in the evening at ten or eleven o'clock and walked along the northern edge of Hyde Park. The streets and houses were indistinct in the blackout. It was double summertime in England, and there was still a glimmer of light coming through the trees of Hyde Park. To my left on the great meadow that begins at Hyde Park Corner, there were the big, white half spheres of air balloons, sitting there like hippopotamuses waiting to be sent up in the air when German airplanes were approaching. To my right were the ruins of the large, luxurious houses that had lined Bayswater Road. The facades still stood with empty windows through which you could see the dark night sky, and rubble was piled up in the front gardens. Sometimes these houses appeared to be the ruins of a large medieval castle or the remnants of a destroyed ancient city. From time to time the faint glimmer of a flashlight indicated that people were climbing around in the ruins looking for treasures among the debris. I felt I had been transferred to a strange past.

I now became reacquainted with the underground, which clearly showed the impact of the war. In descending on the escalator to the train platform I noticed men, women, and children carrying cushions and blankets, and making them into beds along the grim walls of the underground platforms. At the outset I was shocked when I saw hundreds of people cramped together in these dark, airless caves, but after a few weeks I got used to this. Moreover, during my first months in London the number of those seeking nightly refuge in the underground declined. This was a short respite, and the crowds multiplied again when a new weapon, the V-1, a bomb fired from the coast of Flanders, hit English cities.

The night of the first V-1s I was fireguarding our office building for the first time. The alarm bells sounded around midnight and I rushed up the staircase to the roof. I could see no airplanes. The clear signal sounded, and I went back to the second floor where field beds had been set up. I had hardly settled down when the alarm started again. I rushed back up to the roof, and again I saw nothing and returned to the second floor. This game was repeated four or five times. It had not yet been discovered how the alarm system could be adjusted to this new kind of air attack; by the end of August, however, a combination of guns and fighter planes mastered the V-1s.

By then, everyone had become somewhat used to what Churchill calls in his memoirs "the pilotless bombardment." You heard the "doodle-bugs," as they were called, approaching by the noise of their engines; when this noise stopped you knew they were going down, would hit the ground and explode in ten or fifteen seconds. The noise of the engine also indicated how close the bomb was to where you were, and whether you ought to move away from the windows to the middle of the room or from higher to lower floors. One lovely Sunday in September I was walking along Oxford Street, which was crowded with people looking into shop windows or strolling to and from Hyde Park. Suddenly we heard the ominous noise of a V-1; the unpleasant monster, looking like a gigantic, fat cigar, the fire of its engine coming out of its rear, could be seen flying straight along Oxford Street, not even at great height. Everyone wondered when the noise of the engine would stop: before it reached you, when it was above you, or only after it had passed you. When the V-1 was above where you were walking the noisy street became very quiet, and all heads turned upward toward the bomb.

When it had passed, everyone resumed talking with what seemed doubled energy, as if we were coming up to air again after nearly drowning.

There were other, less noisy and less visible indications of how the war dominated life in London. One evening I had supper in a club near our office with some colleagues, among them my friend Hans Meyerhoff. This was not one of the famous London clubs in which intellectuals and the political elite decided what people ought to think and what novels ought to be read. This club on Brook Street was a product of the war, its members mostly Americans who in the privacy of the club could drink as long as they wanted, and who were only too happy to pay a considerable amount of money for solid pieces of meat clearly bought on the black market. I left the club at around twelve with Hans and one of our secretaries. I returned to my rented room, and had just fallen asleep when the telephone rang. It was a much distressed Hans who asked with great urgency to see me as quickly as possible. We agreed that we would set out immediately and meet at a place in Hyde Park equidistant from Kensington, where Hans lived, and Bayswater, where I lived.

When we met, Hans told me that he had accompanied the secretary to her room, also in Kensington, and had stayed for only a few minutes. He had taken along from the office some papers stamped "Confidential" and "Very Confidential" because he wanted to look at them before going to bed. Although it was against regulations, this was not very unusual; we all did it on occasion. The classifications "Confidential" and "Very Confidential" meant very little; only papers marked "Secret" or "Very Secret" contained matters of significance. In any case, before saying good-bye to the young lady in her room, Hans had placed the papers under a flowerpot standing at the entrance to the house. When he returned downstairs the papers had disappeared, and this led to the panicky telephone call. Hans had called me partly because I was then chief of the very small German Section of the London Research and Analysis Branch, and as such had to be informed immediately, and partly because Hans was in need of some friendly comfort. So for several hours we walked around Hyde Park—from the Albert Memorial to the Marble Arch, and on to Kensington Palace. Finally we went back to my room where, with one of us sitting on the bed and the other in a big leather chair— the only chair in the room—we dozed for one or two hours.

Early the next morning we went to the security office of the OSS as soon as it opened. We both had no doubt that, although the papers contained nothing of significance, it would be irresponsible not to report the loss. Hans entered the security office while I sat in the anteroom, expecting to be called in as chief of Hans' section and hoping that I might help by stressing the insignificance of the lost material. After about twenty minutes Hans returned to the waiting room holding what I quickly realized were the papers he had lost. Before he had fully explained why he had come, the American security officer had asked: "Are these the papers you have lost? The British security police brought them to us twenty minutes ago." Hans received a very mild admonition and—dead-tired but relieved—we went to our office. I still don't quite understand how the papers could have been removed in the short time that Hans was in the secretary's room—and it was a very short time because we had parted not very long before his telephone call awakened me. This was one occasion when it became apparent that, although life seemed to go on in normal ways—we used the underground and buses, kept our office hours, ate in restaurants, and went to the theater and to movies—still it was controlled and restricted within boundaries dictated by the requirements of the war.

I gradually became aware that life in wartime London revolved in narrow, circumscribed circles. Schools, colleges, and university institutions, with their staff and personnel, as well as the main collections of libraries, had been moved out

of London. Many English people who worked in London came
to town in the morning but left in the late afternoon for a
place in the country to which their families had been evacuated. If in peacetime the upper classes had been a dominant
feature in London, they were now much less visible; foreigners were now more conspicuous. The English attitude toward
foreigners was very different from what it had been in prewar
London. Foreigners, particularly Americans, were treated with
great warmth, and were even somewhat spoiled as friends
who had demonstrated the excellence of their character by
coming to England's assistance in times of emergency. This
did not mean, however, that the image of the American as
somewhat primitive and rough had entirely disappeared.

At Christmas a colleague of mine and I were invited for
dinner by the family living in a house next to the one where
we were staying, and we decided we could not refuse; our
hosts had been eager to show us their pleasure with our presence in England, and the invitation had been extended weeks
in advance. The family was what the English might call lower
middle class, and it was my impression they felt somewhat
superior to the American colonials. It was by accident that,
probably in continuation of remarks on Dickens' Christmas
tales, the discussion that evening turned to novels, and the
lady next to me could not suppress her utter astonishment
that I had read Jane Austen and Thackeray, and was able to
say something about them. I had the strong suspicion that
she was surprised I could read at all.

Though it was not a time suited to social invitations and
dinner parties, I remember going to two or three evening
gatherings at the house of Harold Laski, a professor of political science at the London School of Economics and a prominent figure in the Labour Party. There the talk, almost always
about politics, was especially interesting because there were
many political refugees present, as well as English people. In
general, however, the military people and civilians of differ-

ent nationalities assembled in London kept rather to themselves. I once spent a long afternoon in York House where
the French met. I was brought there by my friend Etienne
Mantoux, who had served in the French army during the first
months of the war but had managed to come to the United
States after the French defeat. I had gotten to know him in
Princeton in 1941–42. It was a difficult time for Etienne
because, although he felt strongly that he ought to participate in the fight against the Germans, for personal rather
than political reasons he hesitated to join de Gaulle. At
Princeton we had talked a great deal not only about politics
but also about French and German literature; he liked to discuss literary subjects because this was an escape from the
problems of his situation. When I saw him in London he had
joined the Free French, and looked very happy in his blue
French officer's uniform. Indeed, he was a changed person,
full of energy and optimism. He was to be sent to France in
a few days, and we looked forward to meeting again on the
Continent. But in one of the last battles of the war, in the
early days of May 1945 near Würzburg, Etienne was killed—
a confirmation of the old truth that the best of a generation
become the victims of war. His father, Paul Mantoux, has
edited the study of the reparations problem on which Etienne
had been working at Princeton. This scholarly legacy, however, is only a weak reflection of all that Etienne was.

My excursion into the French camp was an exception,
however; my main companions were people working in the
OSS. We had lunch together, usually in the American canteen, and in the late afternoon before supper we had drinks—
usually double gins—in a bar near our office. From there we
often walked to Soho to eat in some French or Swiss restaurant in which the owners had managed to enhance the meager
offerings with attractive trappings. Frequently we returned
to the office after supper to clear our desks.

Life in London was somewhat monotonous. To overcome

the discontent nourished by boredom, there was music, theater, and all kinds of entertainment in abundance. It is my
feeling that London was never as brilliant—neither before nor
after the war—as it was in the last two war years. One occasion that stands out in my memory was a lecture at the Churchill Club, a special organization for Americans serving
overseas. It met on the ground floor of an old, bombed-out
building near the House of Commons. The archbishop of
Canterbury, Cosmo Lang, presided and T. S. Eliot spoke.
His lecture was on Milton, and he set forth—even more sharply
than in his published essays—his well-known critical views
about the combination of art and religious propaganda that
he found in Milton. I was sitting on the floor, perhaps two
rows away from the speaker, and observed that during the
talk the presiding archbishop had his eyes firmly closed and,
if I heard correctly, was breathing rather heavily. Hardly had
Eliot finished, however, when Cosmo Lang rose to say that
he was delighted to hear Eliot's praise for Milton, placing
him next to Shakespeare as one of the two greatest English
poets. I have not forgotten the lesson I learned that evening:
you had better stay awake when you chair a lecture.

Equally unforgettable, although in a very different way,
were the luncheon concerts of Myra Hess. She played in the
National Gallery, which during the war was empty of all its
paintings. The piano stood in the hall that in peacetime had
housed, in its right and left corners, the two Veroneses that
had raised my spirits during my first stay in London. The
concerts were short, but after an hour of Hess playing Beethoven, Schumann, and Brahms, I returned to my office
refreshed and freed from the pressures of wartime London.

The theater had a similar magical effect. Actors and actresses
who in the following decades became known all over the
world—Gielgud, Olivier, Richardson—performed during
these years in London in what was chiefly a classical reper-
tory. I remember seeing *King Lear* and *The Winter's Tale,* a

brilliant performance of *The Duchess of Malfi,* and very fine productions of Sheridan's *School for Scandal* and *The Rivals.* Because of the blackout the theaters played rather early in the afternoon, and you returned to your office in an elevated mood.

Life in wartime London was strangely contradictory. For long stretches it was entirely normal and routine, and then it was suddenly upset by the uncontrollable interferences of war. This tension permeated one's entire life. The British had mastered this tension by clinging tenaciously to routine. Once when a V-bomb exploded nearby, splintering the glass of our office windows, a few minutes later, as always at four o'clock, the housekeeper brought us tea. At the outset the slowness involved in maintaining an ordinary routine in the face of extraordinary events was irritating, but it soon became apparent that this attitude was also an expression of the strength that allowed the English to live through four grim years of siege.

Americans were less able to overcome the tension involved in leading an ordinary life under the shadow of an omnipresent war. Americans were in London only temporarily and provisionally, and their surroundings had only a feeble hold on them. They were restless, and this was especially evident in the decisive final stages of the war. I have mentioned that I often accompanied my colleagues to a bar, usually late in the afternoon, before the evening meal. I don't think we ever got really drunk, but the amounts of gin we absorbed staggers me now when I think of it. This helped us attain for a short time release from the uncertainties of wartime London.

The limitations of life in London became very clear when I moved outside the daily circle. In August 1944 I spent a weekend in Oxford, and early one morning a car arrived to drive me to a meeting at American headquarters in southwest England. It was clear and cool. The sun was rising as we drove through fields and wooded hills that were green and fresh. We passed through a few small towns, the streets still empty, the timbered houses white and clean. I suddenly became aware of what I had almost forgotten: how good life could be.

So far I have said more about the circumstances of life in wartime London and less about the work I was there to do. My work in the Office of Strategic Services took all of my time, and there was something satisfactory about being fully occupied. At my desk in Washington I could never quite silence the doubts about whether our analysis of incoming information, or the memoranda that we composed, made much of a contribution to the outcome of the war. This was not so in London, where I was nearer to the war. I was conscious of being part of a big military machine, even if only a very small part, and the questions and inquiries we had to answer gave us the feeling we were useful.

We were asked to carry out jobs of a varied character: producing a weekly publication, interviewing German prisoners and political refugees, responding to inquiries by American political and military officers. The weekly bulletin was intended to provide information about the general European situation to high-ranking officers (if I remember correctly, to all officers from the rank of major general and up). I must say that this periodical had quite a distinguished staff. Its chief editor was the Harvard economist Paul Sweezy; Arthur M. Schlesinger, Jr., made the various articles readable, and he did so in an admirable way. Once during a half hour while the rest of us were at lunch, he transformed an interesting but complicated, long, and abstract article by Leonard Krieger into a piece that, with none of its ideas lost, was entirely clear and readable. Everyone met to decide on the contents of each issue and its various contributors. In these meetings, which were fairly small, the sharp and critical remarks of Ed Shils kept us firmly on the ground. The group faced a difficult task the day after the failed attempt on Hitler's life, on July 20. We had to explain this event, but we knew only what the Nazis had reported. I think we did rather well in establishing that the conspiracy against Hitler had gone much further than the Nazis had acknowledged. I certainly thought we did better than our Washington office, which tried to brush the event aside.

My interviews of German prisoners of war were aimed not at getting militarily useful information but at finding out about the situation inside Germany, and about the "mind of the German people." These interviews only confirmed what I knew: that until very recently the Germans had lived rather well, chiefly through exploitation of the occupied countries. The war had had a relatively small impact on most Germans, with the exception of those who lived in the large cities that were targets of bombing attacks, and even this was only a recent phenomenon. I also interviewed refugee politicians from the Eastern European countries the Nazis had occupied and the Russians were now "liberating." Our discussions were based on assumptions, which turned out to be illusory, that some kind of democracy would be allowed to develop in these countries, and turned on the question of what could be done to support such developments.

One of my interviews was with a politician of whom I had heard much in the preceding twenty-five years and whom I was most anxious to meet and talk to: Count Karolyi, who for a few months in 1919 had been president of the Hungarian Republic and had initiated the division of Hungary's large estates among the peasants. He was living in what I remember as a small house or apartment in Hampstead, but he was still the great gentleman with an interested if distant attitude toward the contemporary scene. It was an intellectual pleasure to get his point of view, and I saw him several times. He was one of the few who had no illusions: he was sure that the fate of Hungary would be in the hands of the Russians.

Much of our time at the OSS was consumed with responding to requests for factual information coming from military

or political quarters. I was involved in two tasks of this sort
that had some slight impact on later developments.

Early one morning I received a telephone call requiring me
to report at nine o'clock to a building that, I believe, belonged
to our embassy. There I met a colleague of mine from the
Geographical Section of the OSS and a third person who, I
believe, was a British officer. We were told that by midday
the European Advisory Council wanted to have a plan for the
division of Berlin among the three occupying powers: the
United States, Great Britain, and Soviet Russia. The instruction we received was that there ought to be a small central
district the three powers would occupy together and from
which they would govern Berlin, and that each of the three
separately occupied sections should be contiguous to this central section. We mapped out an area around Unter den Linden as the common zone; of course, this part of our work
soon became a victim of the growing tension between East
and West. We discussed whether each of the occupying powers should have a harbor in its section, which some higher-
ups had suggested, but this idea seemed hardly to fit Berlin's
geography. The areas surrounding Berlin would be in the
hands of the Russians who could block the passage of any
ship they wanted. We thought it important, however, that
no one power alone have access to and control of the large
Tempelhof Airfield. The east and north of Berlin seemed to
us the appropriate zone for the Russians, and accordingly we
assigned the west and the south to the British and the Americans, respectively. The lines we drew have stood ever since,
although later a French zone was carved out of the British-
American area. In the course of these discussions one incident
gave me great pleasure. When we had to decide which parts
of the west and south should go to the United States and
which to Great Britain, I pointed to the Grunewald and Dahlem area on the map and jokingly said: "This is where my

relations had houses; this ought to be the American section," and this was accepted.

I mentioned before a pleasant August drive through the English countryside from Oxford to the American headquarters. I was summoned because information was needed on a political issue, namely, the treatment of Nazi party members and Nazi adherents after our entry into Germany. I was received at the American headquarters by an army colonel who in civilian life had been in charge of the police force of a large Midwestern town. He was to command the police in occupied Germany, and he showed me a memorandum he had received from Washington. This memorandum, which as I found out much later had been written by Herbert Marcuse in the Washington office of the Research and Analysis Branch of the OSS, suggested that 220,000 Nazi officials be arrested immediately. The colonel was greatly relieved when I agreed with him that this was not feasible. There would not be sufficient personnel to carry out these arrests, nor was it easy to imagine where, and how, this endless number of prisoners could be securely detained. It was simply impossible to arrest all the members of the chief Nazi organizations as the Washington document had envisaged.

Thus we began to pare down the list of those to be imprisoned, restricting it to key officials: the officers and noncommissioned officers of the principle Nazi organizations. In this form the document became part of the famous Joint Chiefs of Staff Order 1067, laying down rules for de-Nazification. I would say that neither the colonel nor I had the feeling that we were doing more than reducing the recommendation that had come from Washington to a manageable level. We certainly did not anticipate the vehement dispute that later erupted about whether this part of 1067 was too harsh or too mild. I learned from this episode that when working in a large bureaucratic apparatus you should be careful about what you set down on paper, because you can never know what will become of it—although I think in this particular case perhaps the result was not entirely bad.

This visit to the American headquarters took place on a beautiful day. This was the summer of our landing on the Continent, the conspiracy against Hitler, the reconquest of Paris, and our advance to the German frontiers. I suspect that these events had some influence on my impression that this summer was an uninterrupted sequence of lovely, sunny days. This summer I began to love London.

Chapter VII

Interlude

AFTER Hitler's last gamble—the Battle of the Bulge—had failed, the invasion of Germany from east and west proceeded rapidly. It became merely a question of time when the whole of Germany would be occupied by Allied forces. Work in the London office of the OSS Research and Analysis Branch now focused almost entirely on problems connected with the coming occupation. We knew that immediately after the end of hostilities we would be transferred to headquarters in Germany. A good part of our office staff—particularly those who had worked on France—were already in Paris, and in March 1945 the rest of us were ordered to join them where we could get firsthand information about the situation in Germany more quickly and easily. We were stationed in Paris from the middle of March until May 20, when we were flown to Wiesbaden, the headquarters of the OSS in Germany. Although nobody would admit it, we had little to do in Paris: the two months preceding the move to Wiesbaden were an interlude.

This interlude was important for me, however, and I remember certain events of this period with particular clarity. For a long while we had lived a circumscribed life, narrowly focused on a few issues. Now there was a sudden relaxation of pressure, and our concerns were no longer limited to what the next day would bring. With the most urgent danger over, we could think again about what was important to us, and what we wanted to do with our lives.

I

WHEN early in 1944 I had left the United States for London, I had not expected that I would return to the Continent, particularly not to Germany. While I was in Washington it was generally believed that German-born members of the American intelligence forces would not be used in the occupation; this was said—whether truly or not I don't know— to have been a decision by the highest quarters. Accordingly, while in London I assumed that upon the removal of the office to the Continent I would be sent back to the United States. I was thoroughly content with this prospect: I did not want to go to Germany. The great majority of Germans whom the Nazis had forced out were unwilling again to enter into close contact with Germany and Germans. Indeed many German refugees refused to set foot on German soil for years after the war. Originally I shared this reluctance to enter Germany. (I might mention here that my sister, who was teaching German literature at the University of London, did not return to Germany until ten years after the end of the war.)

In the forty years that have passed since the end of the war I have been frequently in Germany. I was a guest professor at the University of Cologne for an academic year, and I have participated in several meetings and conferences in Germany.

I now find my original reluctance to return difficult to understand, but it probably was the result of a combination of rational and emotional factors, some of them contradictory. I hated the idea of hearing the explanations and excuses of those who had remained in Germany, and perhaps had even served the Nazi government. Whenever people have begun to explain and apologize for what they did in Germany during the Nazi period, I have cut them short. I don't like seeing people humiliate themselves, and in my opinion there was simply no excuse. My image of Germany in 1945 was also strongly influenced by notions widely accepted during the preceding years, according to which Nazism was an outgrowth of the German past, so that Nazis and Germans were identified. I was always aware of the crudeness of this picture, but because we then had only incomplete knowledge of the working of the Nazi power apparatus, of its inescapability, and of its relationship to the German social structure, one was inclined to place greater emphasis on this explanation of the rise of the Nazis than one would now. Perhaps, however, the reason for my reluctance to re-enter Germany was simpler. After having worked hard to cut myself off from the past, I shied away from the stress involved in seeing the past come to life again.

As my work in London became increasingly concerned with the problems of occupation, my attitude began to change: I became anxious to know how the plans for Allied occupation would work out. I continued to say, however, that I really did not want to go to Germany. When I was told that it was considered desirable that I should continue as section chief in Germany, I complied but I made a condition: that before going to the Continent I would have a vacation. Thus, in late March 1945 I spent a few days in Oxford. I stayed at a grubby little hotel near the railroad station. I can no longer recall in detail what I did: I slept late, read, looked in bookshops, inspected college buildings, and visited friends. I met Gustav

Mayer, the biographer of Friedrich Engels, with whom I had become acquainted in London in the early thirties. Mayer told me that his sister was married to the philosopher Karl Jaspers, which I had not known, and that he had not heard from them for several years. He urged me to make contact with them, and, if at all possible, see them.

One experience from this week in Oxford that I recall vividly was an invitation to lunch from B. H. Sumner, the warden of All Soul's College. After the lunch, when the other guests had left, he suggested that we take a walk in one of the college gardens. As we were looking at the green grass that was just emerging, Šumner asked: "How would it affect us if the sky were green and the grass were blue?" This playful, rather donnish remark aroused in me a response Sumner could never have imagined. I realized that intellectual life begins only when you are free to choose the questions on which you want to work, and they are no longer prescribed to you by others.

II

I THEN joined my colleagues at the Paris headquarters of the OSS, which was situated on a side street of the Champs Elysées. On arrival I was told that all the rooms were occupied, and that I should sleep in whatever room became vacant when its occupant had night duty. I had limited enthusiasm for sleeping every night in the bed of a different person, and without asking permission—because what I intended was in all likelihood against regulations—I decided to rent a room elsewhere. The value of the dollar was then so great that I found one without difficulty. It was a kind of self-contained one-room apartment with its own entrance from the central corridor hall on the ground floor of an apartment house in the rue des Saints-Pères. The room was large, but it had scarcely any furniture and inadequate light. In bed at night I used a flashlight to read John Hersey's *A Bell for Adano,* which had just come out, and mused about the differences between Italian Fascism and German Nazism, and between liberation and occupation. (My reading therefore could be regarded as being in the line of duty.)

The main advantage of the room was its location. On my way to the office in the early mornings I walked along the rue des Saints-Pères, over the pont du Carrousel, and passed through the Louvre and its courtyard to the underground, which took me—gratis, because I wore an American uniform—to the Champs Elysées. Crossing the pont du Carrousel I could see the facade and the towers of Notre-Dame on the right; on the left I had a glimpse, I thought, of the Arc de Triomphe, and all around me was the baroque exuberance of the Louvre. There was little traffic, and the streets were almost empty; all I saw seemed to be there for my personal delight. Every morning was an overwhelming and exhilarating experience; a world that had seemed lost in frightful cruelty, barbarism, and starvation had reemerged.

III

TOWARD the end of April we received a report that the archives of the German Foreign Office, which during the last years of the war had been moved out of Berlin, had been discovered in a castle in the Harz Mountains. I was ordered to go there and find out whether the report was correct. I was accompanied on this trip by my friend and colleague in the OSS, Leonard Krieger, who drove the jeep. The first evening and night of the journey we spent happily in Luxembourg, which was strangely untouched by the war and where we ate better than we had in months. Then we entered Germany, driving rapidly along the autobahn, frequently detouring over fields or dirt roads in places where the surface of the autobahn had been demolished by bombs.

The first large German town we entered was Kassel. All
the reports I had read of the destruction brought about by
saturation bombing had not prepared me for what I encountered. In certain parts of the town hardly a house was standing; none was undamaged. The street on which we drove was
nothing but a path cleared in a field of rocks and rubble.
However, when we reached the industrial section a large factory, which had produced locomotives in peacetime and tanks
in wartime, was still standing. We were told that tanks had
been rolling out of this factory until the day American forces
had taken the town. Many of us—I among them—had har-
bored doubts for quite some time about the efficacy of mass
bombing. We believed it strengthened the hands of those in
power because they alone had the facilities to order the most
urgent repairs, to supervise and control communication, to
provide food, and to move people out of town; the great masses
of the population were deprived of any possibility of joint
action that might have ended Germany's senseless resistance.
This skepticism seemed confirmed by the success of Nazi officials in keeping the tank factory functioning. Despite the
shock the sight of the destroyed city gave us, we left Kassel
in high spirits. While driving through the town we observed
that people—mostly American army personnel—were eagerly
reading the army newspaper that had just come out. We
grabbed one: Mussolini had been captured and executed. The
end seemed much closer.

From Kassel we drove to an army camp where we stayed
one or two nights. The building in which we were billeted
was on a hill, and until recently it had been occupied by the
Nazi guards of a forced labor camp in the valley below. Now
we had put the Nazi officials into this prison camp, and the
Eastern European forced laborers were employed as cooks and
waiters in the American canteen on the hill above. We felt
like superior beings playing with the fate of inferiors according to our whims. Then we drove to Naumburg. I was eager

to see the cathedral and its celebrated statues again. But the area was closed off, and after a look at the outside of the cathedral we drove on to Weimar, where, on a green before Goethe's famous garden house, American soldiers played baseball.

We spent that night in Leipzig, which at this time—before the Allied military commands had settled in the occupation zones and withdrawn their troops from adjacent zones—was under American control. Leipzig was our last stopping place before we set out for the castle in the Harz Mountains. We were warned to be careful in the mountains, parts of which had not been entered by American or English troops, and might still harbor Nazi troops in the forests. However, we encountered no one on the roads, which wound through lovely, peaceful mountain scenery. At the castle the officer in command of the American forces received us in a friendly but sober manner; the day before, some of his troops had been wounded in the fighting that was still going on between the Harz Mountains and the Elbe River. We ended the day early, spreading our sleeping bags on the floor of one of the many large rooms of the "new" castle.

The next morning we entered the older, original castle, which was no longer habitable. We were accompanied by a British colonel who had the same mission we did. The old castle was a towerlike building, dark and humid. There we found hundreds and hundreds of volumes filled with documents scattered around in a bewildering jumble. I grabbed a few of them to examine their origin, and one of the first I looked at contained papers from the 1860s, some of them signed by Bismarck. There was no doubt that, with the exception of papers from the last years of the Nazi regime, the castle contained the entire Foreign Office archives. Having put together a report about the "treasures" in the castle, we returned to the new castle. While we were eating our meager evening meal the officer in command of the American troops appeared, holding three glasses and a bottle of Madeira: German radio had just announced that Hitler was dead. Thus we celebrated the end of the war.

Having accomplished our mission, we started back to Paris. After crossing the Rhine we drove along the autobahn on the hills overlooking the Moselle Valley. For anyone who has grown up in Germany the Moselle Valley—praised in poems and celebrated for its wines—has a romantic enchantment. I had never been there and I wanted to see it. I said to Krieger that since the war was over it would not matter if we wasted a few hours, and so we left the autobahn and drove down into the Moselle Valley, and then along the river. The valley seemed untouched by the war. The villages were clean and intact. Children ran out of the houses and stared at us. Everyone looked at us with curiosity; they had never seen an American uniform or an American jeep. Later we realized that we had seen no able-bodied men, only children, women, and very old men. At points where the road crossed the river, the bridge was destroyed; at these places we found ferries whose attendants were only too happy to offer their services. In this valley so remote from the present, a ferry seemed the appropriate means of transportation. The sun was shining, the trees had fresh leaves, and bushes and flowers were beginning to bloom. The hills were still brown, but full of vines. As in the past there would be a wine harvest. No reason why 1945 should not be a good wine year.

Chapter VIII

Germany 1945

I

ON MAY 20, 1945, the entire German Section of the European Research and Analysis Branch of the OSS was flown from Paris to Wiesbaden. Our offices and canteen were located in Henkel's champagne factory, and we were housed opposite the factory in a cluster of villas whose owners had been moved out. On the ground floor of the largest of these villas were common rooms—a living room, a dining room, a kind of bar, and a billiard room. In the evenings we spent much time playing billiards or, in favorable weather, playing croquet in the garden. The bar was popular in good and bad weather; it was not unusual that one or another of us had to be helped upstairs to bed. Our drinking demonstrated the validity of the law of supply and demand. We hardly paid attention to the champagne, which was available for free; instead we pre-

ferred to drink wine for which we had to pay. One reason
why billiards, croquet, and drinking played such a great role
in our lives was that this was the period of nonfraternization—we were not permitted to have social contacts with
German civilians. Consequently we were thrown entirely on
ourselves; we were together with the same people from morning to evening. It was in some ways like being in a prison.

Insofar as official duties demanded, members of the Research
and Analysis Branch had permission to interview Germans,
but these interviews were businesslike and formal; they were
not meant to—nor did they—establish human contacts.
Because of the lack of communication with the German population, a middle-aged German who spoke passable English
and whom the administration of the OSS had employed as
bartender in the central villa of our "colony" was immensely
popular. We liked to listen to his descriptions of how awful
life under the Nazis had been. Suddenly he disappeared, and
it emerged that he had been high up in the SS. This episode
strengthened those who favored strict observance of the nonfraternization order.

Life in the Wiesbaden headquarters was a kind of shock.
After the excitement of the war and the rushing events of the
preceding months we suddenly felt cut off from the main-
stream, dropped on a remote island. We felt at a loss, a feeling that was reinforced by uncertainty about what our job
was. "To observe and to report" was officially our task, and
in the special case of Germany this meant seeing to what
extent the principles laid down in the various occupation
handbooks had been followed. Where possible, we were to
assist in carrying them out.

Conditions in Germany, however, were very different from
what had been envisioned in the occupation guides. Nothing
was stable; everything seemed in flux. Driving through the
country we encountered processions of women, children, and
elderly men who had been evacuated during the war and were

now tramping back to their homes. Others were fleeing the feared Russians, looking for a place to settle. After some weeks German soldiers also began seeping back. We never knew what we would find at the place we were ordered to report about. Extended sections of larger towns had been destroyed, but some of them like Heidelberg and Baden-Baden had been spared and still looked exactly as they had at the beginning of the century. Some of the smaller towns and villages were badly damaged; in others, the houses still had the white-washed, solid aspect of prewar times. There was no postal service, and no trains were running. Communication among towns and villages was difficult, if not impossible. Under these circumstances our isolation in the champagne factory had its advantages. It was a relief to be able to shut out for some hours the troubling and disquieting questions raised by our surroundings.

The chaotic situation in Germany made restoration of the bare necessities of an orderly life the most urgent task. The rebuilding of roads and houses, the repair of sewers, of water, gas, and electricity lines, the reestablishment of communications that would allow provision of food and transportation of building materials: all had the highest priority. These tasks required the skills of local Germans, who quite unavoidably would assume a leading role in the local administration.

All this was not only unforeseen in the planning of the occupation, it was even in contradiction to the notions that had dominated the thinking in Washington. Government and administration, even on the lowest level, were to be in the hands of the occupying powers. Employment of Germans was to be considered only after an investigation to ensure the exclusion of all those who had been Nazis. I might remark here that the Germans themselves were so eager to denounce former Nazis that, although Germans moved much more quickly than had been foreseen into responsible positions of local administration, in my opinion very few former Nazis

were among them and not many mistakes were made. However, the notion that for a while Germans ought to be excluded
from participation in the organization of their political life
had its roots also in the conviction that they ought to be "re-
educated." After the end of the Nazi regime a "political pause"
was considered to be necessary. The Germans were not to be
allowed to form political parties, to edit newspapers, or to
embark on political activities of any kind.

Suggestions that had been made in Washington, particularly from the Research and Analysis Branch of the OSS—
that the German trade unions might be useful in the political
re-education of Germany—turned out to be illusory. The
destruction of factories, the very slow, limited resumption of
economic life, and the impossibility of establishing contacts
beyond the area in which one lived made this impractical.

The contrast between the views prevailing in Washington
and the actual situation in Germany was for me typified in
what happened when we had our first visit by a man from the
Washington office. When he had recovered from his flight I
offered him a drink, and, standing before the fireplace, he
said at once: "The people in Washington are not at all satisfied with what you are doing." I cannot deny that I was pleased
to read in the memoirs of Lucius Clay, the head of the American military government in Germany, that in the early stages
of the occupation a major problem for him had been that the
policy directives he had received in Washington had shown
little awareness of the actual conditions that existed in Germany at the end of the war.

In the course of affairs another reason emerged why the
plans made in Washington proved to be unfeasible. The
American zone was only one of the zones into which Germany
had been divided. What happened in the American zone could
not remain uninfluenced by what went on in the other zones,
and the policies followed by the various occupying powers in
their respective zones differed greatly.

I became very much aware of the difference between the American and French zones when in the early summer of 1945 I drove down from Wiesbaden to Freiburg, in the French zone. Nonfraternization with Germans was still a strict rule in the American zone, and I was highly surprised when the young French officer attached to me took me to a restaurant where we were happily served by German waiters and German cooks. This French officer invited me to a reception that evening. When I arrived, there were a large number of people assembled, French officers and well-to-do Germans. Among them were the French commanding officer and the German mayor of Freiburg, whom the French had appointed; they greeted each other with brief, friendly speeches. Then we all mixed in conversation and later there was dancing. Of course, there was a purpose behind the benevolent treatment of the German population in the French zone; it was still uncertain at the time whether German unity would be maintained or whether Germany would be divided into a number of independent states, among which there might be a southwestern state tied to France.

In the eastern part of Germany the Russians pursued their own line. In their zone political activity was not only allowed but encouraged: newspapers appeared written and edited by Germans, and political parties were formed, among them a very active Communist Party, which tried to expand toward the West. News about these activities in the French and Russian zones soon spread in the American zone, and it was clearly unavoidable that American occupation policy would have to adjust to a certain extent to what was going on in these other zones. Though it can be assumed that active participation by Germans in the administration and the revival of political life would have taken place relatively soon in any case, these developments were certainly accelerated by the practices of the other occupying powers.

The most important deviation from previous planning was

the failure of the victorious powers—the United States, Great
Britain, France, and Russia—to carry out what they had previously agreed upon: to establish a common administration
for the whole of Germany. Shortly before the Potsdam Conference, in July 1945, I participated with members of the
OSS in a meeting convened in Wiesbaden by Allen Dulles,
the head of the OSS in Europe, to put together a list of names
of Germans whom the American government might propose
as members of an all-German government. It was a beautiful,
mild evening, and it was delightful to sit on a terrace with a
view sloping down toward the Rhine Valley. Among Dulles'
staff was Gero von Schultze-Gävernitz, whom I had last seen
at a costume ball in Berlin fifteen years before. We both were
amused at being reunited in such different circumstances.
The meeting was for the most part agreeable, although opinions sometimes clashed. I encountered sharp opposition when
I spoke against placing on the list of candidates the name of
Gottfried Treviranus, former minister in the Brüning government. He seemed to me too much of an old-style conservative. The next day one of those present at the meeting
said to me: "You always seemed a very flexible person; I did
not know you could be so doctrinaire."

I have outlined the situation in the American zone during
the first five months of occupation—the months I was in Germany—in very general terms in order to show that there was
no clear line, no definite policy, no special function assigned
to the work of our office. Actually our work consisted largely
in giving information and advice to American officers who
relied on our expertise to help them accomplish their special
assignments. I had my hand (I use this expression intention-
ally to avoid giving the impression that I had any influence
in determining policy) in two issues that loomed quite large
on the agenda of these first months in occupied Germany: the
reopening of the universities, and the revival of political life.

II

ONE of the often-proclaimed aims of the occupation was the "re-education of Germany," and in this the universities were of central importance. Originally it was thought that the universities ought to remain closed for a lengthy period to allow the removal of Nazi professors and the investigation of professors whose teaching and attitudes had indicated approval, or at least acceptance, of Nazi doctrines. As it soon emerged, however, there were compelling reasons for a quick reopening of the universities. Young men, some of whom had been conscripted into the army only in their last school years, were now returning to a country in which they could not easily find employment. It seemed better to give those who had passed the necessary examinations a chance to study and prepare for a career than to have them on the streets. This raised the further question of the extent to which the preparation in Nazi-directed and Nazi-governed schools had patterned their thinking and whether measures ought to be taken to counteract their conscious or unconscious Nazi habits of mind. The suggestion was made to introduce something quite novel at German universities, namely, a general preparatory course somewhat like the introductory courses at American colleges. This introductory course would extend over almost all fields of knowledge, acquainting students with the views of the world outside Germany and arousing a critical sense about what had happened in Germany. Only after students had passed this course in their first semester could they proceed to more specialized studies.

Edward Hartshorne was the official in charge of education in the American zone and he considered this question of the reopening of universities of great importance. At his suggestion I went to Freiburg in order to report to him about educational policy in the French zone; and I made several trips to Heidelberg, the most important university within the American zone. Heidelberg was where a reopening of academic life in the American zone would have to start, not only because of its tradition and reputation, but also because it was undamaged.

In Freiburg, the outward signs of occupation were much less visible than in the American zone. In accordance with their generally benevolent occupation policy, the French had permitted the reopening of the university, and they had some justification for this decision. Freiburg had always been a rather conservative university, a feature reinforced by the presence of a Catholic theological faculty and a strong Catholic element in the other faculties. Because of the politically right-wing inclination of many Freiburg faculty members, there were relatively few dismissals after the Nazis came to power; moreover, the election of the pro-Nazi philosopher Martin Heidegger as rector in 1933 had further assured the Nazis that Freiburg University would keep in step. Since the faculty, because of its conservative character, had remained more or less intact during the war, it contained few fanatical Nazis who had to be dismissed. Many of the conservative professors had even managed to maintain a certain distance from the Nazis, and toward the later years of the Nazi regime an opposition group with contacts to a center of the resistance, the Goerdeler circle, had developed among the Freiburg professors. The professor of modern history, Gerhard Ritter, whom the Nazis had imprisoned as a dangerous conspirator, had just come back after an adventurous escape over the Elbe from the Russian zone, which he described happily.

In discussions with various members of the Freiburg faculty I tried to explore what they thought about the idea of a general course for all students in their first semester, and whether the course could be introduced in all the universities within the Western zones. Most professors welcomed the idea, but they also raised questions that made me aware of the obstacles that stood in the way of any planning that went beyond local arrangements. Some of these conversations in Freiburg touched on other matters as well. I had been talking about the question of a general introductory course with a professor of the law faculty when he said to me: "Professor Heidegger will visit me tomorrow; I am sure he would like to talk to you, and if you are still here, perhaps you could come and we might continue this discussion with him." I returned the next day and Heidegger was there. Our discussion was not very fruitful: Heidegger agreed eagerly to whatever we were suggesting. The professor of law remarked that in the planning of such an introductory course he would place emphasis on the Christian foundations of European thinking, and turning to Heidegger he added: "You probably would place greater stress on the classical foundations of our thought." Heidegger responded: "Oh, not at all; for me too Christianity is the basis of our intellectual endeavors." It did not occur to Heidegger that the American officer who was participating in the discussion had read his famous work *Sein und Zeit (Being and Time),* and was therefore aware that his remark was aimed more at satisfying what he expected the American attitude to be than expressing his basic philosophy.

During another meeting the director of the university library was showing me the library when I noticed that people were carrying books from the cellar to the upper floor, and from the upper floor to the cellar. I asked him what these people were doing, and he responded that they were returning to the shelves books that the Nazis had forbidden and that had been locked up in the cellar. I smiled and said: "But they are not only taking books upstairs; they are also taking books downstairs." He replied: "Those are the books you have forbidden us to read." Now *he* smiled.

The situation at the University of Heidelberg was different from that at Freiburg. Heidelberg had been a bulwark of republican and democratic thought during the Weimar

Republic, and many of its professors were either forced to retire or dismissed outright soon after the Nazis came to power; their places were taken by enthusiastic Nazis. Many of the professors who had been prematurely retired had survived the war and were around when I visited Heidelberg. I talked to a good number of them, including Gustav Radbruch, who had been minister of justice in the German government under a Socialist chancellor; Gerhard Anschütz, the author of the authoritative commentary of the Weimar constitution; and the sociologist Alfred Weber, brother of Max Weber, whom I visited several times. At this time Germans had no means of corresponding with England, and Alfred Weber asked me to help by sending the manuscript of the book he was writing to England, where it was published in 1947 under the title *Farewell to European History*.

Together with a colleague I visited the philosopher Karl Jaspers, to whom I brought news about his brother-in-law in England. As we were leaving, Jaspers asked me whether I could come back again in the afternoon—alone. Of course I agreed, and when I returned Jaspers told me that he and other former professors from Heidelberg University had been drafting a constitution for the university. He was aware that this document would have to get the approval of the occupying authorities, and he wanted my opinion as to whether an expression they had used would be acceptable. He read to me a sentence stating that the aim of the university was the formation of an aristocracy of the spirit (*geistesaristokratische Ordnung*). Jaspers wondered what impression the term "aristocracy" would make. My answer was simple and direct: the term "aristocracy" ought not to be used in the document, and indeed, as I later heard, the formulation was changed.

During my meeting with Jaspers I read the entire draft of the constitution. In the past Heidelberg University had had no constitution, but it was understandable that now the professors whose careers had been cut short by the Nazis were anxious to revive the great traditions of the past, and to set down in a document the principles that would guarantee the maintenance of intellectual values and scholarly research, and prevent subjection of the university to the dictates of politics. I had expected that the draft would take precautions against political interference by the government. I was astonished, however, to discover that the document was also directed against any influence the students might exert. It was particularly concerned with eliminating their participation in appointments to the faculty and in determining the contents of the curriculum. This was a reaction to the role students had played under the Nazis, particularly during the first years of the regime. Nevertheless, it was striking the degree to which the draft made the faculty autonomous and envisaged a return to an unchanged, pre-Nazi situation.

In discussions with younger intellectuals in Heidelberg I found out that they were not enthusiastic about a return to the old tradition and were skeptical that such a restoration could last. However, they felt that under current circumstances the reopening of the university, particularly of the medical faculty and the law faculty, was of primary importance and should not await needed reforms.

In the course of the summer of 1945 it became increasingly clear that the universities in the American zone had to be opened as quickly as possible, both to train people in the professions and to provide the same educational opportunities that existed in other zones. So the idea of mandating a general introductory course for all university students was dropped. I cannot claim that my activities in this field of educational policy had any positive results, but I enjoyed my visits to Freiburg, and most of all to Heidelberg.

It was a delight to escape the grim scene of Germany in ruins and to come to Heidelberg, lovely and unchanged. The OSS office in Heidelberg was located in a pleasant house, somewhat up a hill, with a view down on the town. One of

the people I called on was Theodor Heuss who lived in a very
small ground-floor apartment in the suburb of Neuenheim. I
had met Heuss in Berlin when he was teaching at the Hochs-
chule für Politik, and we talked about acquaintances of that
time. As I was leaving, Mrs. Heuss also began to leave for
town, where some public event marking a first step towards
the reestablishment of self-government was about to take place.
I told Mrs. Heuss that I would be glad to take her into town
in my jeep. Since this was still the period of nonfraternization, Mrs. Heuss was surprised and accepted my offer with
alacrity. What astounded me was that instead of sitting down
in the jeep she remained standing and waved to the people
we passed on the way into town. They responded with
applause. I cannot deny that I felt somewhat uncomfortable
as my gesture of politeness was transformed into a demonstration of German-American friendship.

III

A DECISIVE reason for the gap between the planning for the
occupation of Germany and its implementation, beyond the
actual conditions in Germany, was foreign policy, in particular the beginning of America's tensions with the Russians.
With the collapse of the idea of a common administration
over the whole of Germany, and with the steadily increasing
political activity in the Russian zone, the pressure to remove
restrictions on German political activity in the American zone
became irresistible. Our section was concerned with observ-
ing and reporting these developments; I was actively involved
only twice, and in a very minor role.

When the American authorities decided to allow the publication of newspapers in their zone, they stipulated that the
newspapers be edited by a team representing different political views. Theodor Heuss was suggested as one of the editors
of a newspaper called the *Rhein-Main Zeitung*. One morning

I received a telephone call from an American intelligence officer who was involved in the arrangements. He told me that the colonel whose approval was required had strongly objected to the presence of Heuss on the editoral staff of this newspaper. He asked me to come to Homburg or Nauheim (I have forgotten which) to try to explain to the colonel that his objections to Heuss were unjustified. I talked to the colonel for several hours. His chief argument was that Heuss had written for the *Frankfurter Zeitung* and that, during the Nazi period, the *Frankfurter Zeitung* had been a particularly insidious and dangerous instrument of Nazi propaganda: it had given the outside world the impression that a certain amount of freedom existed under the Nazis. I argued that in order to attain the propagandistic impact that in his opinion the *Frankfurter Zeitung* had had, the newspaper had had to publish articles that were not in complete conformity with the Nazi creed, or that had been written by authors who were not thought to be Nazi sympathizers. In short, not everyone who had written for the *Frankfurter Zeitung* was a Nazi. Moreover, I pointed out that it had been difficult for people known to be unsympathetic to the Nazi regime to earn money, and for these people writing in a newspaper was a way to do this. The colonel finally gave in, and I felt proud of what I had achieved: the *Rhein-Main Zeitung* appeared with Heuss as one of the editors. In one of the early issues of the paper he published an article, "The German Army," which emphasized that, despite the condemnation of Prussianism and militarism, the army had had its virtues. It was a sensible article, but not prudent: one hardly expected to find a defense of military virtues in a newspaper that the occupying powers had allowed to appear only after lengthy debate, especially since the order to remove all military literature from libraries was still in force and remained so for quite a while. Heuss' article defending the German army was something of an embarrassment. My reputation for having a special faculty for distinguishing good Germans from bad Germans suffered a severe blow.

The last, but in many respects also the most interesting, political event I attended in Germany in 1945 was the meeting of the Social Democratic Party in Hanover. From the outset it was a somewhat dubious enterprise. The various zones of occupation were still strictly separate and any conference bringing together inhabitants of different zones was officially forbidden. On the first day of the conference delegates from the British zone gathered in an open meeting, whereas in order formally to comply with regulations, the next day's meeting, at which delegates from all over Germany were present, was a closed session. Since communications and transportation for Germans were still difficult and unreliable, the presence of delegates at the closed meeting was rather haphazard. Some areas were unrepresented, while others were overrepresented, and an important factor in attendance was previous acquaintance with those who had arranged the conference, especially Kurt Schumacher, who was the moving spirit behind the meeting.

The great surprise, almost the sensation, of the conference was the arrival of five delegates from the Russian zone under the leadership of Otto Grotewohl. In the closed session there quickly developed a clash between the comrades from the East and those from the Western zones. One issue in dispute was whether the central office of the Socialist Party, if the party emerged on a national level, should be located in Berlin, as it had been in the past, or in the West. There was vehement discussion also about whether strict adherence to Marxist ideology, particularly to the notion of an unavoidable class struggle, was still appropriate under present circumstances. In the course of this discussion the Western Socialists criticized the controlling influence the Communists wielded over the Socialists in the Eastern zone, and the Socialists from the East in turn complained about the dependence of the

Western Socialists on the occupying powers in *their* zones. Despite its noticeable bitterness, the discussion seemed somewhat unreal because the United States, Great Britain, Soviet Russia, and France were referred to only as "the occupying powers." They were never directly named and accused. Finally, one of the delegates made the mistake of saying "Russian" instead of "occupying power," and the British officer in charge immediately got up and closed the meeting.

Afterward I had private talks with Otto Grotewohl and Gustav Dahrendorff from the Eastern zone, and a very long conversation with Kurt Schumacher, the leader of the Socialists in the Western zone; after the establishment of the German Federal Republic Schumacher became the leader of the Socialist Party. He was an impressive person, full of energy and ambition despite a physical handicap that was the result of punishment by the Nazis and ten years in a concentration camp. He stated very frankly his primary concern: the Social Democrats should not again commit the mistakes they had made in the Weimar period. They had to broaden their base beyond being purely a workers' party, and they had to abandon Marxist ideology, particularly the notion of the class struggle. In all this Schumacher anticipated the course the German Social Democratic Party would take in the Federal Republic. He presented his ideas with a vehemence and an authoritarianism I did not like. There was no doubt that he was driving with all his force toward a break with the Socialists in the Eastern zone. Such a break might have had to happen under any circumstance, and in a general way his approach may have been right. But in the somewhat fluid situation that then existed, I had doubts that the West should initiate the break. Moreover, in order to absolve the Socialists of an accusation that had been made in the past—that in their internationalism and pacifism they had neglected German national interests—Schumacher showed a very nationalistic outlook. He emphasized that there could be no real cooperation with the victorious powers as long as the Germans were not allowed to be masters in their own house—as long as Germany was occupied. The great importance he attached to the past political mistakes of the Socialist Party astounded me. It seemed to me that he was still living in the world of Weimar.

It was probably unavoidable that the elimination of the Nazis brought into the forefront people who still lived in their memories of Weimar. I was struck with how this longing for a return to the past expressed itself at the Hanover meeting. Outside the meeting places there was a large tent; the long tables within were decorated with red flags and set with coffee pots and cups. On the back wall was a large photograph of Karl Marx. During the Nazi period the executives of the Socialist Party, with its chairman, Erich Ollenhauer, had gone to England. They used the occasion of the Hanover Conference to return to Germany for this first time since the war. The Hanover meeting became the celebration of a reunion, of a coming together with old friends, of an exchange of old memories. The conference seemed to me much more like a meeting of Socialists in a garden restaurant after an excursion on the first day of May than the occasion for a new beginning.

IV

I CANNOT recall feeling overly disturbed or emotionally upset at being in Germany again: I did not want to get involved in German affairs, and the circumstances of my stay—living apart from German daily life, being in contact with only a very limited number of people, being primarily concerned about "our" zone, which was only a small part of Germany—facilitated keeping a distance.

I felt a strong interest, however, in learning what had happened to people I had known—in part out of curiosity, but also to help if friends were in straitened circumstances and finally to test my own reactions to the reemergence of my past.

I rediscovered personal bonds and connections soon after my arrival in Germany. On the way from Wiesbaden to Freiburg we drove on the autobahn along the Rhine. As we drew near Baden-Baden, I asked the driver of the jeep to turn into the town because I was curious to see how it looked now. When we entered Baden-Baden we discovered that the main road was closed; Lattré-de-Tassigny, the commander of the French army in this area, was in town and a troop review was taking place. We took a side street through an area that was very well known to me, but my attention was fixed on the French soldiers standing at every corner, giving directions which I translated for our driver. Suddenly a soldier moved into the middle of the street indicating that it was closed, and we could not advance farther. To reverse our course the driver turned sharply into a driveway. When I looked up, in front of us was the house that had belonged to my parents, and in which I was born. It had been sold after the death of my father, but since the new owners were friends of my mother, I knew it well. It had been built by Weinbrenner, a well-known German architect in the early nineteenth century, and in 1945 it looked exactly as it had in the past. When I saw the house again in 1985, it had been modernized and, at least in my opinion, had lost its charm.

In the chaotic situation that existed in postwar Germany, where people had moved from one place to the other, where there was no mail, no telephone, no up-to-date directories it was difficult to contact people you wanted to meet or to get information about them.

In the course of the summer of 1945 a State Department mission, led by an American diplomat, De Witt Poole, came to Wiesbaden with the task of interviewing German diplomats. American officials were beginning to develop an

absorbing interest in the activities of the Russians, and the
purpose of Poole's mission was to find out about Russo-Ger-
man relations in the years before Germany's invasion of Russia. I had known Poole at Princeton, and because of my
knowledge of German he had requested that I be temporarily
assigned to his mission. When I looked through the list of
German diplomats who had been assembled in a special camp,
and whom we were to interview, I discovered the name of
my friend Heinz Trützschler von Falkenstein. I had last seen
him in the summer of 1933, when we spent a day together
in Lucerne. Since I am a traditional historian and believe that
what you can learn from documents is more reliable than
what people tell you, my enthusiasm for interviewing these
German diplomats was limited. Thus, I persuaded Poole to
give me the job of working out an exact organizational chart
of the German Foreign Office under the Nazi foreign minister
Ribbentrop. For this I needed the collaboration of one of the
German diplomats, and I got Trützschler assigned to assist
me. So for a few days we sat together in a small room, working on our chart and also exchanging memories of former
times. He told me what he had done during the Nazi period,
and this helped answer a question that had puzzled me: how
someone who was not a Nazi could live through those times
in Germany and remain decent without being heroic. Trützschler told me that after Germany had left the League of
Nations he had been taken into the German diplomatic service, but managed to keep a distance from the Nazi regime
by remaining in lowly positions of bureaucratic administration. Trützschler's record was such that without difficulty he
was able to continue his career in the diplomatic service of
the Federal Republic. He retired with the rank of ambassador.

Such encounters were a happy accident, however. I was not
always so lucky in my inquiries about former friends or
acquaintances. While in Heidelberg I read on a list of former

faculty members who were still alive the name of a professor whose daughter I had greatly admired when we were both students in Munich. I thought no harm could be done by interviewing the father and inquiring what had happened to his daughter. I had hardly entered his study when he presented me with a number of memoranda on plans for a territorial reorganization of Germany, and our discussion turned immediately to the problems of the present. It was an interesting discussion, but it provided no opportunity for personal questions, and I left without knowing what had happened to his daughter. Some weeks later I read in one of our newspapers that he had been appointed to a high position in the administration of the American zone, and we met again after that in the building in which he had an office. I was waiting in the hall, rather conspicuous in my American army uniform among a mostly German crowd, when the door opened and he appeared, saying good-bye to a visitor. When the professor-administrator saw me, he opened his arms, saying: "My dear Captain Gilbert, you certainly should not have to wait in this hall," and with many bows he ushered me into his office. Evidently he believed that my visit with him in Heidelberg had exerted influence on his appointment. I did not feel it appropriate to tell him the true reason for my visit: to find out about his daughter. I never got this information.

There was one place, however, where I knew I would get news about a good number of people whom I had known in former times: that was Berlin, and I was sent there for a few days in October 1945.

Colleagues at the OSS who had been in Berlin had told me that whatever you saw in other parts of Germany, you would be utterly shocked by the devastation of Berlin. Still, I was not prepared for what I saw, or almost physically felt, immediately upon my arrival at the airfield. The air I breathed seemed different; the war was still close around you. Berlin had not just been the target of bombing attacks; the city had

been a battlefield. Remnants of destroyed tanks could still be
found on the streets, and destruction was everywhere. In the
center of town not a house was intact, entire facades were
smashed, and one could see into the rooms in which people
were still living. Lack of food, lack of heating material—
disasters that in the Western zones still lay ahead—were already
harsh facts in Berlin. On the day after my arrival I was walking in the center of town when suddenly there passed a train
of horse-drawn carriages loaded with guns and guided by
Russian soldiers. It was hard to believe that in this motorized
age an army—and an army that had defeated the famous German army—still used horse-drawn wagons. The presence of
the Russian soldiers, with their impenetrable peasant faces,
reinforced the impression that we were still at war; with the
best will in the world it was impossible to evade the impression that with the Russians an alien, inaccessible element was
entering the life of Berlin.

Berliners were only too eager to make clear their affiliation
with the Western world by dwelling on stories about the
barbarism of the Russians. Again and again they told of the
Russians' raping of German women, and there is little reason
to doubt the accounts of violence, brutality, and cruelty that
accompanied the last stages of the battle for Berlin. It was
much more difficult to establish the accuracy of rumors that
such atrocities were still going on in outlying districts and
surrounding areas. Edward Hartshorne, with whom I had
worked on the reopening of the German universities, tried to
establish the facts. Hatshorne had done some research in Germany before the war and had gotten to know Meinecke and
his family; although Meinecke himself was still in Göttingen, his daughters were in the family house in Dahlem, and
Hartshorne arranged through them to interview some women
who could report on what was going on. Hartshorne asked
me to come along. I cannot say that our interrogation proved
much of anything; it was almost impossible to penetrate the

layers of rumor and hysterical fear and get to the facts. One of the purposes of interviews of this kind, however, was to show that attention was being given to the problem, and thereby to calm the fears and excitement that nourished an atmosphere of tension and might lead to desperate actions. I mention these interrogations not because they were of particular significance, but because the very fact that discussions of rape and violence went on in Meinecke's living room, with its furniture unchanged since prewar times, seemed to me to symbolize the end of a world in which I had once lived.

Not only the terror of the war, but also the horrors of the Nazi regime were still present in Berlin. I visited the parents of my friend Dietrich Bonhoeffer. Only a few months before, in April 1945, two of their sons and two sons-in-law had been executed by the Nazis. We assembled around a table: the parents, two of their widowed daughters, and a married granddaughter with her husband. I could hardly say anything, and could only admire the strength they showed in talking to someone whose presence must have reminded them of a very different past.

One afternoon and evening stand at the center of my memories of Berlin in 1945. It was then still possible to move around freely in all parts of the city, and I had decided to go to a performance of Brecht and Weill's *Dreigroschenoper (Threepenny Opera)* in the Eastern zone. I had been told that it was the same production with some of the same actors I had seen in the 1930s. In the early afternoon I received a telephone call from an American official who asked whether I would be interested in seeing a film that had delighted Hitler: the trial and execution of the conspirators of July 20. The film was being shown to a small group that afternoon for the first time since its recent discovery. (Since then it has been frequently shown, although, I have been told, only in abbreviated form.) In October 1945, among the ruins of Berlin, the events depicted in the film had not yet become a part of history, but still possessed a terrifying immediacy. The shouting of the judge, the accused desperately groping to keep up their trousers (their suspenders had been taken away from them) but still managing to be quiet and dignified, the horrors of the execution—all this was hardly bearable to see. To go directly from this film to a play seemed almost frivolous, although it was a way to get one's thoughts away from the frightfulness of these images and to regain some balance. The way to the theater required all my attention. I entered the underground, which moved smoothly along for three stations, but then stopped because a stretch of the line had been destroyed. I climbed out of the train over some rickety stairs and wooden planks, and then walked along a street, some of its houses in ruins but others, as flickering lights showed, inhabited. Then I entered the underground again and traveled a few more stations. All this happened three or four times before I finally reached the theater. The play began. Indeed, there were still many of the same actors, the same balletlike moves, the same interplay of passion and greed, of corruption and loyalty, of contempt and respect for bourgeois morals—all that had once enchanted me. But if I had once found a cheerful light-heartedness in the play, an optimistic undertone that society would inevitably become more fair and more just, I now felt little of this hope in the darkness of postwar Berlin. I realized that I had not changed the world; the world had changed me. Were there still links with the world that had been and in which I had grown up? This question was probably the right preparation for finally doing what I had wanted to do since my first hours in Berlin, but had not yet gotten around to: seeing what had happened to the house in which I had grown up.

Postscriptum

A HISTORIAN— perhaps even more than other writers—is aware that the writing of memoirs is different from writing a historical book. The writer of memoirs is less concerned with what actually happened than with the emotions, the thoughts, perhaps even the actions that an event inspired. Of course, he will try to check the correctness of his memory, to make sure that the time and the place of the event to which he refers are exact. I soon discovered how easily memory can go astray. Dr. Barry M. Kātz of Stanford University, who has been working on the activities of the OSS in wartime, was kind enough to give me copies of some of the memoranda which I wrote in the summer of 1945. I was amused and astonished to discover that I remember well and correctly the contents of my interviews and activities, but that I was frequently wrong about the date on which they had taken place.

Some of them had occurred weeks earlier, some of them weeks later than I had thought.

In preventing such mistakes the comments of friends and colleagues who were kind enough to read the manuscript, or parts of it, were invaluable. But their comments—their criticisms and their approvals—had for me still greater importance. When you are writing a book of a very personal character you frequently feel unsure whether something of interest to you can be of interest to others; on the other hand, a story which, for some personal reasons you find highly interesting, might seem to others quite irrelevant. Moreover, doubts about the value of writing reminiscences never disappear, and friends are crucial in dispelling them. Arnold Haase Dubosc, Christoph and Flora Kimmich, David C. Large, Arno Mayer, James J. Sheehan, Arthur R. G. Solmssen, and Fritz Stern were kind enough to read the manuscript. I am deeply grateful for the attention which they gave to it, and I hope they will notice that I made full use of their comments.

Without the encouragement of Donald Lamm of W. W. Norton & Company, I might not have undertaken to write a whole book of memoirs. I wrote the first chapter when, after an operation, I was unable to go to my office and to libraries and to continue the historical research on which I had been engaged. Donald Lamm's reception of those first pages encouraged me to continue. Steven Forman of W. W. Norton was an indefatigable editor of the manuscript. I wish to thank Robert Kimber for providing an English version of the German letters of Chapter V. Roxanne Heckscher of the Institute for Advanced Study seemed not only never to tire of typing the various versions of the manuscript, but her interest in what she was typing helped to keep me going.

Last but not least, it must be said that my wife, to whom the book is dedicated, exerted decisive influence on the content and style of the manuscript and her interest dispelled many of the doubts and hesitations that I had in writing and publishing such a personal book.

I found there is a certain satisfaction in writing memoirs. In the course of time you notice with increasing irritation the gaps in knowledge of the past which those born after you show, and you find a certain pleasure in having a part in countering this trend. Moreover, when you get older the future occupies a smaller place in your mind, and you enjoy less thinking about the future than you enjoy thinking about the past.

Index of Names